IMAGES
of America

LONG BEACH ISLAND

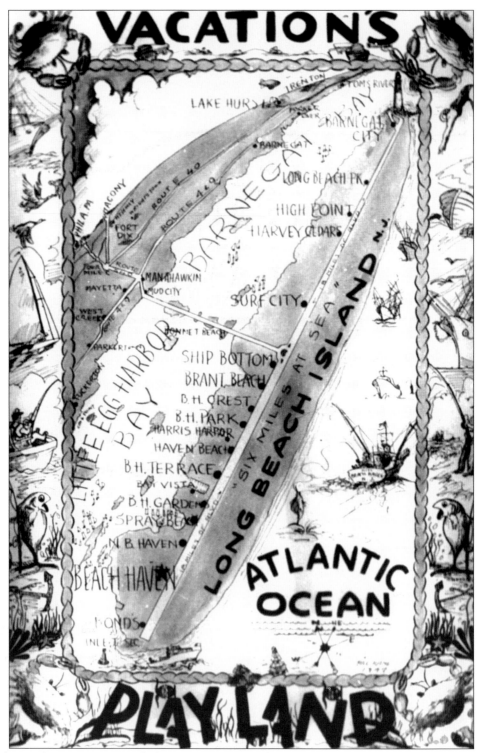

This early picture postcard shows a caricature map of Long Beach Island, described as "Vacation's Playland."

IMAGES
of America
LONG BEACH ISLAND

George C. Hartnett and Kevin Hughes

ARCADIA

First published 2004

Published by Arcadia Publishing,
an imprint of Tempus Publishing Inc.
Portsmouth NH, Charleston SC, Chicago,
San Francisco

Printed in Great Britain

Library of Congress Catalog Card Number: 2004101180

For all general information, contact Arcadia Publishing:
Telephone 843-853-2070
Fax 843-853-0044
E-mail sales@arcadiapublishing.com
For customer service and orders:
Toll-free 1-888-313-2665

Visit us on the Internet at www.arcadiapublishing.com

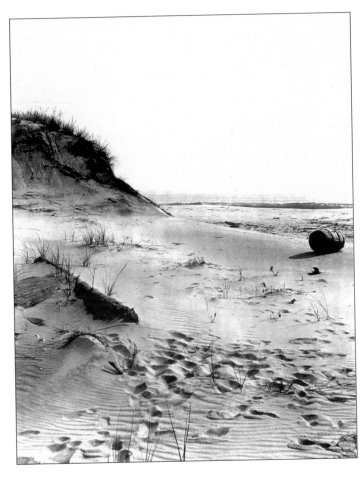

Shown here is a peaceful image of the unspoiled beaches of Long Beach Island c. 1900.

CONTENTS

ACKNOWLEDGMENTS

Our endeavor to portray the life and times of the people of Long Beach Island through vintage photographs would have been impossible without the help of our family and friends. Their loving support and assistance in assembling a collection such as this is greatly appreciated. It is through these early images (collected by author George C. Hartnett) that we can trace how the area has grown and changed through the last 100 or so years.

We wish to thank Yolanda and Alexander Hartnett Sr., parents of author George C. Hartnett, for instilling in him the love of Long Beach Island. The Hartnett family history goes back over 100 years on the island, and we were happy to include family photographs in this history. We also thank Alex Hartnett, Esq., for his assistance with the book.

Thanks also go to Carrie Hughes, wife of the author, Kevin Hughes, for her invaluable assistance in editing our text and for her great support in the writing of the book, and to the author's sons, Davey and Evan Hughes, for their patience, support, and love.

We would like to dedicate this book in memory of the many local historians before us, namely John Bailey Lloyd. His important work in recording the history of Long Beach Island will help future generations learn about the past. We also dedicate this book to the memory of the author's sister, Florence Bernard Hartnett.

—George C. Hartnett and Kevin Hughes

INTRODUCTION

Long Beach Island is indeed a treasure on the Jersey Shore with its white sandy beaches, warm sun, and cool ocean breezes. This 18-mile-long barrier island is located along coastal New Jersey in southern Ocean County, separated from the mainland by the beautiful Barnegat Bay.

The history of Long Beach Island (or LBI, as it is commonly known today) began back in 1609. The area was first charted by the famous explorer Henry Hudson in his ship's log entry dated September 2, 1609. Here he described a "great lake of water," which was actually the Barnegat Bay. The "mouth of the lake" as he described it, is better known today as the Barnegat Inlet. He noted a "natural island," which of course would become Long Beach Island. Years later, in 1614, Capt. Cornelius Jacobsen Mey, a Dutch navigator, traveled down the coast of New Jersey from New Amsterdam (New York). Upon reaching the northernmost tip of the island, he noted the dangerous shoals marking the inlet. He named these waters Barendegat, which roughly translates into "inlet of the breakers." Much later, on a 1769 survey map of "the Jerseys," Long Beach Island was then known as Old Barnegat Beach.

The very first tourists at Long Beach Island were most likely Lenni Lenape Indians. Long before Henry Hudson or Captain Mey ever visited the area, American Indians were known to have visited and, at times, lived there. American Indians took their seasonal pilgrimage here each year from their inland Jersey homes. The spring and summer provided an opportunity to take advantage of the great fishing, hunting, and clamming on the nearby barrier islands. At the time of the first white settlers, New Jersey had an estimated American Indian population of around 10,000. When early settlers arrived in the area, they paid the American Indians for their land, even though many arrived here with prepared royal deeds and grants laying claim to the property.

The first documented white settlers arrived on Long Beach Island c. 1690. Most came from the already established towns on the mainland. A handful settled in at Great Swamp (present-day Surf City) and also Harvey Cedars, both located at the northern end of the island. These brave men began to hunt whales off its shore. Whaling at this time was practiced from as far north as Long Island down to the Jersey Shore. The North Atlantic Greenland, or right whale, as it was commonly called, provided a source of whale oil and baleen, or whalebone, valuable commodities of their day. Whales had to be spotted from land. Small wooden boats were rowed out into the surf, and the whales were hunted down. A harpoon was used to spear the great whale, and after being killed, the whale would be towed to shore. By the 1800s, several whaling stations were established on the island, and 12 families were considered permanent residents of Long Beach Island. This was the beginning of the colonization of LBI.

The whaling industry eventually died out c. 1830, as the whales vanished from the local waters due to overhunting. The locals adapted, and soon hunting and fishing would become their primary industry. Through the years, visiting hunters and fishermen would come and would, of course, require lodging. Hotels began to spring up along the length of the island to satisfy their needs. The waters surrounding LBI remained quite treacherous, with dangerous shoals located just offshore. Hundreds of shipwrecks took place off Long Beach Island, and something had to be done to prevent this. An early light was built at Barnegat Inlet in 1834, making it only the fourth such light on the entire Jersey coast. A newer and much brighter light replaced this one in 1858. Several lifesaving stations were also built to rescue seamen from the shipwrecks offshore. More and more people came to the island to settle. In addition, the area noticed an influx of seasonal visitors, who found the fresh air and setting quite desirable. The idea of establishing first-class seaside resorts went from the planning stages to fruition.

From its humble beginnings, Long Beach Island eventually grew to include over 20,000 year-round residents, living in over 20 separate towns. Thousands of seasonal and weekend visitors now also visit the island we call Long Beach and enjoy the very same pleasures that the first tourists, the American Indians, enjoyed.

One

HUNTING, FISHING, AND SAILING

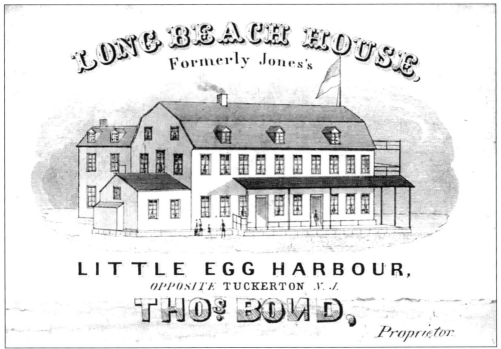

This is an early business or trade card, c. 1860, advertising the Long Beach House on the southern tip of the island. Built in the early 1800s, the hotel was a favorite of early hunters and fishermen who came from Philadelphia and as far away as New York. Purchased in 1851 by Thomas Bond, it was operated on this site until c. 1885, when a few newer and more modern hotels were built in nearby Beach Haven. The building was demolished c. 1909.

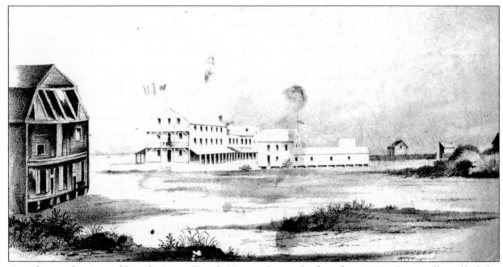

Another early view of Bond's Long Beach House shows the hotel c. 1880. Originally called the Philadelphia Company House back in 1820, it quickly became a famous Jersey hostelry, providing lodging, food, and entertainment to hunters and socialites alike.

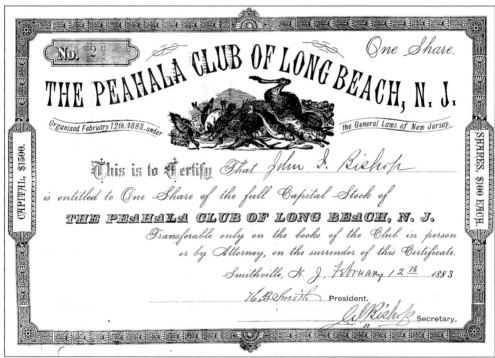

The Peahala Club, one of the many hunting and fishing clubs to come to Long Beach Island, was built in 1882 by a group of New Jersey hunters. It stood around present-day 90th Street in Long Beach Township. It encompassed over eight blocks of oceanfront property and remained a popular sportsmen's club up into the 1930s. Shown here is an early stock certificate for just one share of the club, certificate No. 2, dated 1883.

LBI has always been known for its prime fishing grounds, and at one time, it was known as the fishing capital of the Northeast. Beach Haven in particular was a magnet for game fishermen and boaters. Tuna and other big game fish were favorites of both the local anglers as well as visiting island guests.

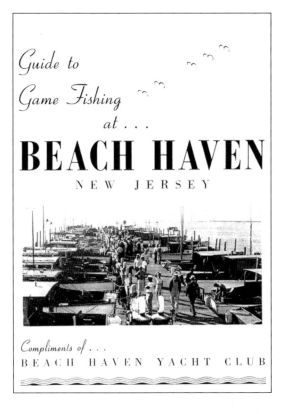

Guide to

Game Fishing

at . . .

BEACH HAVEN

N E W   J E R S E Y

Compliments of . . .

B E A C H   H A V E N   Y A C H T   C L U B

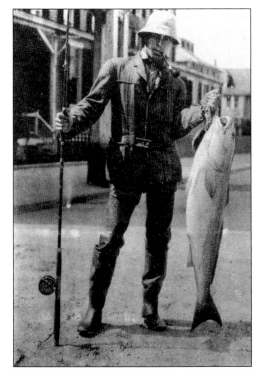

The catching of a large channel bass or bluefish was always a photo opportunity. Here, a man shows off the one that did not get away, caught in the surf off Beach Haven.

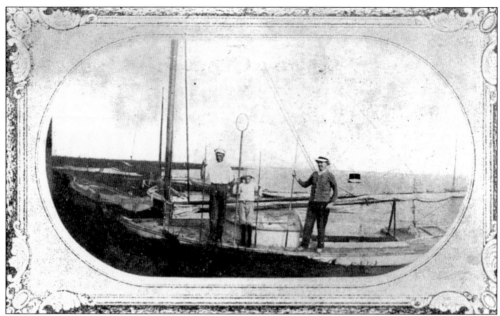

Crabbing was another favorite pastime of the islanders. Crabbing required simple gear, including a piece of string, a net, and a bunker or a chicken leg. One would simply wade into the bay, throw out the hand line, and wait for the crabs.

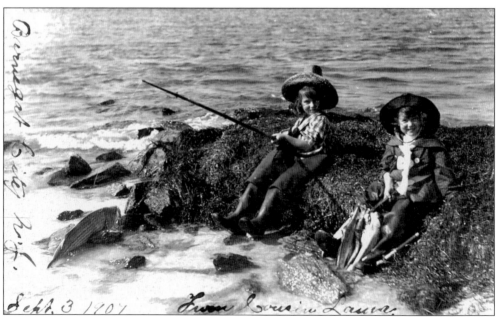

In this 1907 view, two young girls pose on the rocks near the old Sunset Hotel in Barnegat City (later renamed Barnegat Light). They show off the day's catch.

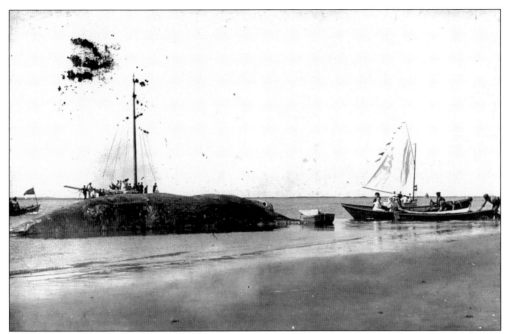

Here is a rare image of a whale aground at Beach Haven c. 1909. Whaling began in the 1600s on LBI and was a source of valuable whale oil and whalebone. A dangerous life, whaling was reserved for the strong and brave, who often battled mammals that weighed up to 60 tons.

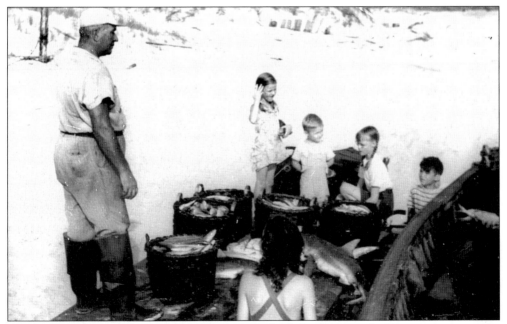

Children often loved to watch the fishermen unload the day's catch. This is an image of a pound fisherman at Captain Bohan's Fishery at Haven Beach sorting the different types of fish into wicker baskets.

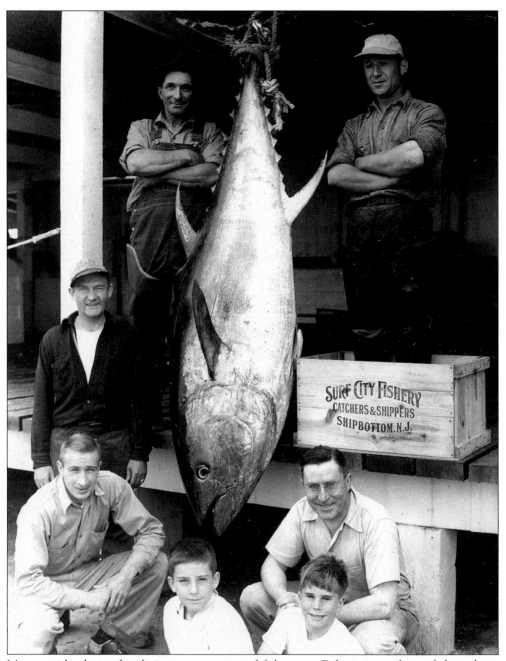

Many an islander made a living as a commercial fisherman. Fisheries were located throughout the island, where fish were sorted, cleaned, and processed for shipping to major markets in the tristate area.

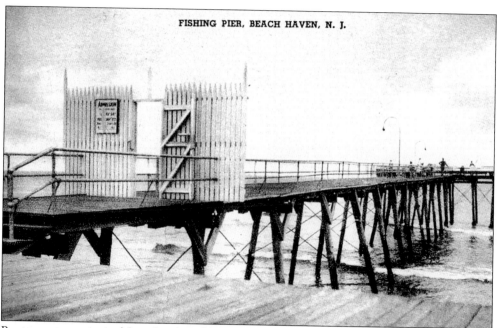

FISHING PIER, BEACH HAVEN, N. J.

Boats were not required for a fun day of fishing. Several fishing piers were built, jutting out into the Atlantic Ocean, allowing people of all ages to enjoy saltwater fishing.

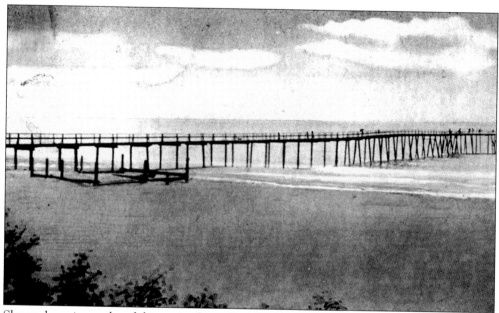

Shown here is another fishing pier located in Beach Arlington (present-day Ship Bottom) c. 1920. These piers would later fall victim to the great storm of 1944.

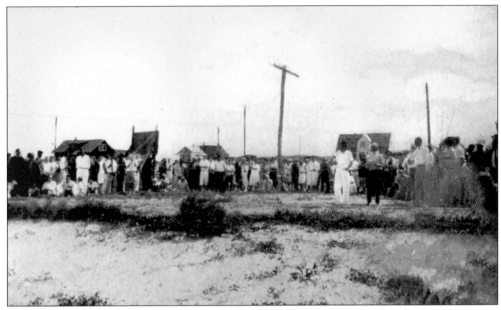

Fishing was a means for relaxation, but it could also be taken very seriously. Many competitions and tournaments were held, with the largest fish caught bringing both prizes and bragging rights. Pictured here is a surf casting tournament at High Point.

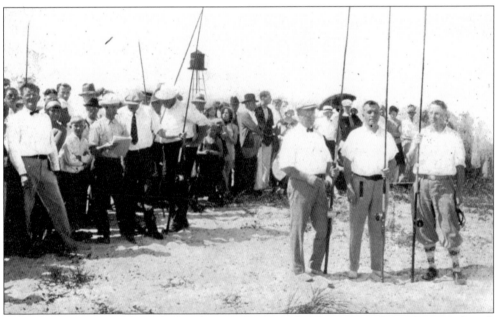

Surf fishing was enjoyed from the beach, with the entire family enjoying the surf, sun, and sand. In this view, proud fisherman pose at High Point.

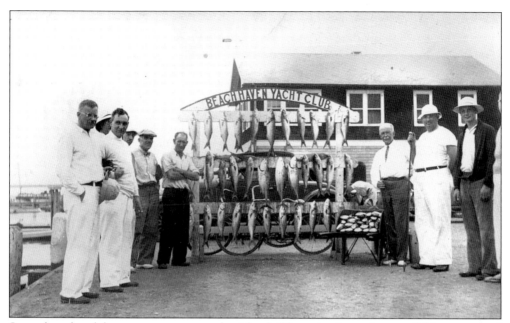

Several yacht clubs sprung up across the island. They also hosted many fishing trips and competitions, as shown here *c*. 1935.

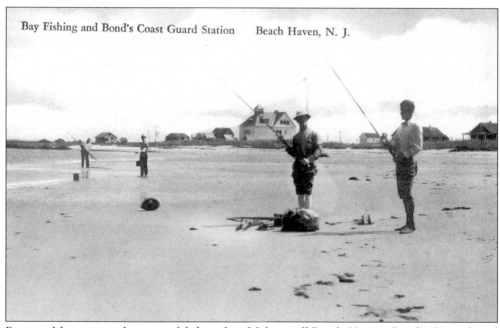

Portrayed here is another peaceful day of surf fishing off Beach Haven. Bond's Coast Guard station can clearly be seen in the distance.

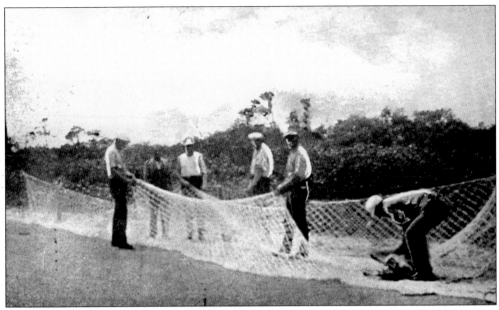

Finishing a day of commercial fishing also meant maintaining your equipment. Repairing your nets, which were often cut by rocks and other sharp objects, was a necessary chore. These men are repairing their nets at Beach Arlington.

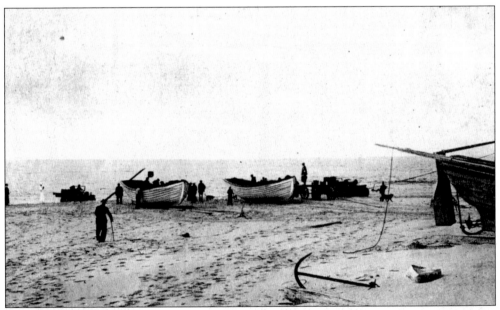

A pound fishery is shown here c. 1935. Wooden boats holding the day's catch are pulled ashore, and the many fish are loaded into splint baskets. Busy fisheries were found in Barnegat City, High Point, and Beach Haven.

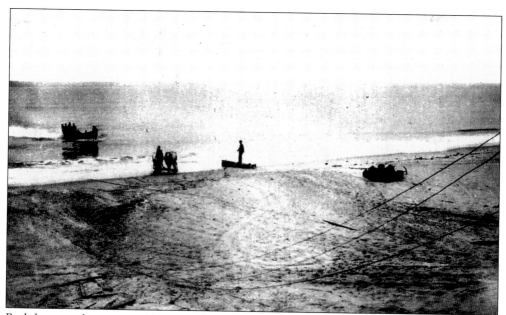

Both horse and wagons and later mechanical vehicles were used to pull the heavy pound boats through the surf and up onto the beach. Seen here are the fisherman working off Beach Arlington, or Ship Bottom.

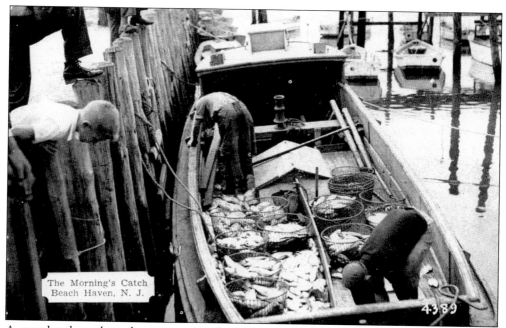

The Morning's Catch
Beach Haven, N. J.

4389

A crowd gathers along the pier to view the freshest seafood possible. A good honest living was made by fishing the bay and ocean off Long Beach Island.

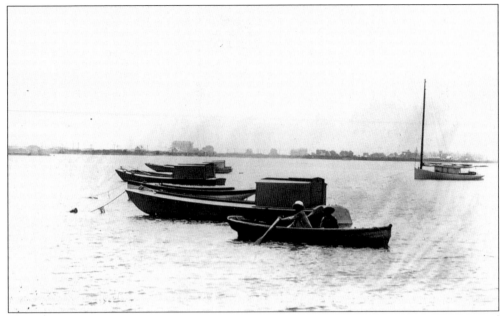

Pleasure boating was another popular pastime on both the ocean and Barnegat Bay. Rowing and sailing made for a fun day out for the summer tourists. Here, people row by several hunting and fishing boats and pleasure yachts near Beach Haven Terrace.

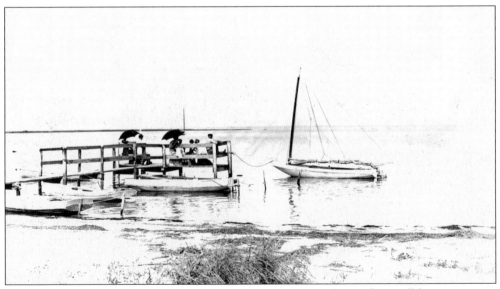

Small docks such as this one in Beach Haven Terrace were a haven for small boaters to rest, stretch their legs, or watch a beautiful LBI sunset. Umbrellas provided protection from the bright summertime rays of the sun.

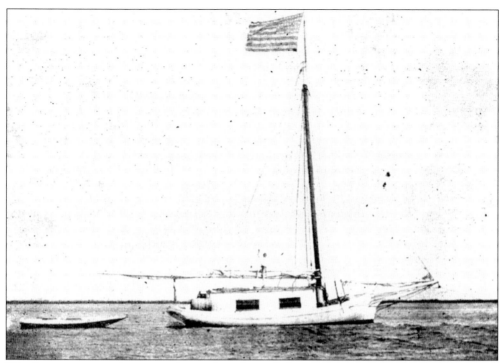

Wooden cruising or pleasure yachts such as this sailed up and down the Jersey coast, bringing the affluent from as far away as New York. The many yacht clubs catered to their needs.

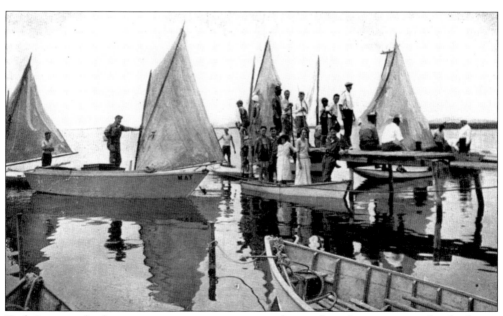

Yachting was also known as a competitive sport, with prized trophies given out for the fastest entry. Popular yacht clubs were located in High Point, Beach Haven, and Spray Beach. This gathering took place at High Point.

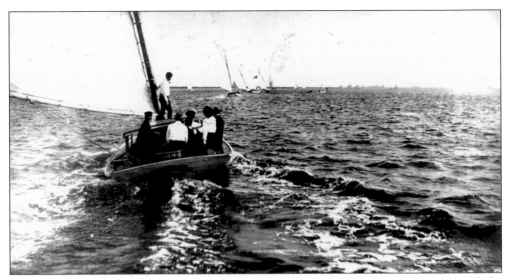

Sailboats such as these were used for daytrips around LBI, often including a picnic lunch for excursionists. The Barnegat Bay was an ideal location for smooth sailing.

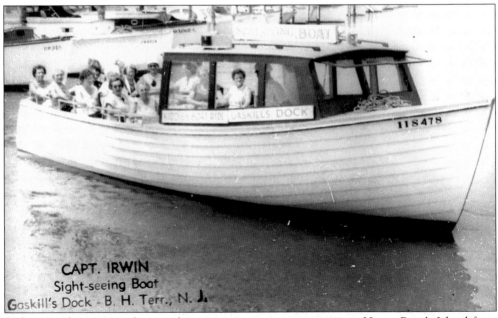

CAPT. IRWIN
Sight-seeing Boat
Gaskill's Dock - B. H. Terr., N. J.

Sightseeing boats were also popular, giving visitors a unique view of Long Beach Island from the water. Many old ship captains enjoyed their semiretirement, chartering their boats out to tourists.

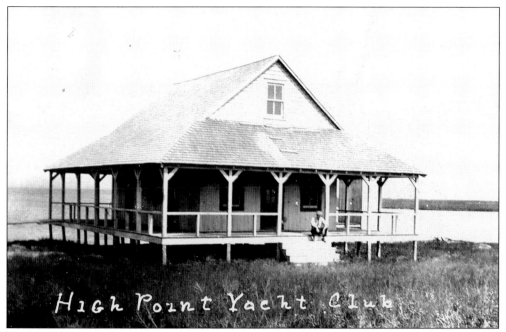

The High Point Yacht Club stood at the northern end of Harvey Cedars. Buildings such as this hosted visiting sportsmen and boaters and provided shelter from the elements. This view dates from *c*. 1912.

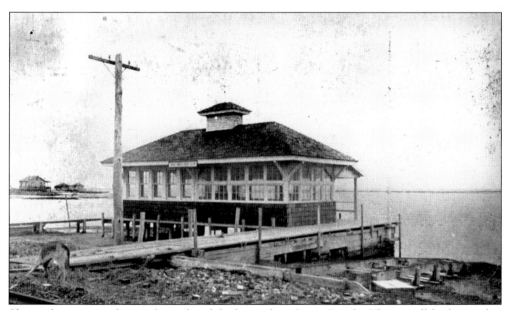

Shown here is another early yacht club, located at Spray Beach. These well-built wooden structures withstood many great northeasters.

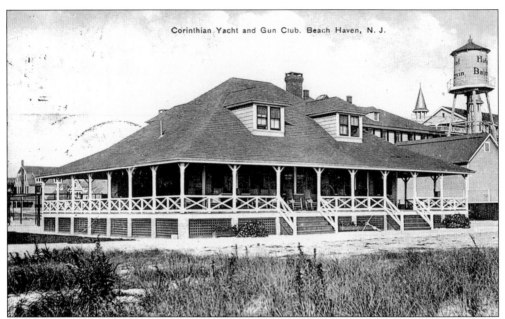

Located next to the famous Hotel Baldwin, the Corinthian Yacht and Gun Club was built in 1904 at the corner of Marine Street and Beach Avenue in Beach Haven. It attracted the social elite, who attended trapshooting competitions, dances, and other social events.

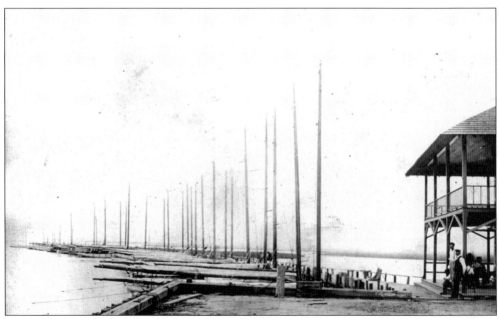

The major competitor to the Corinthian Yacht Club was the much larger Beach Haven Yacht Club. Established in the 1880s, it came into its heyday in the 1920s and 1930s with record numbers of active members.

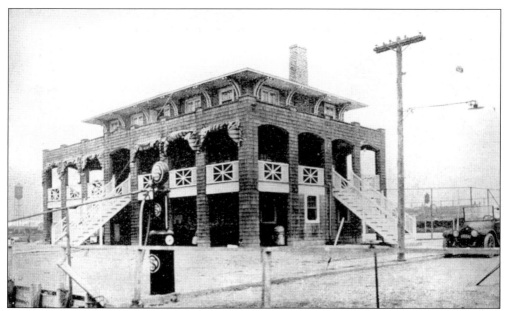

Here is a unique piece of classic Jersey Shore architecture, the Little Egg Harbor Yacht Club at Beach Haven. Shown here *c.* 1925, it also served small boaters' needs by providing fuel via an old glass-topped gasoline pump at the dock's edge.

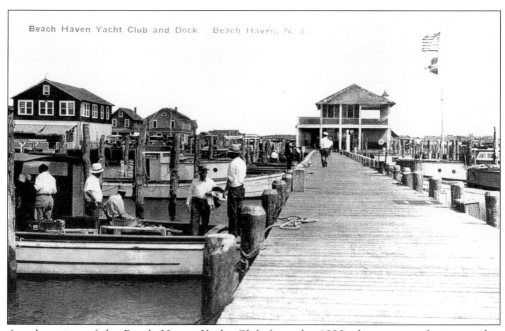

Beach Haven Yacht Club and Dock   Beach Haven, N. J.

Another view of the Beach Haven Yacht Club from the 1930s shows rows of nice wooden pleasure boats and cruisers. The dock was known as the place to gather with friends and discuss the news of the day.

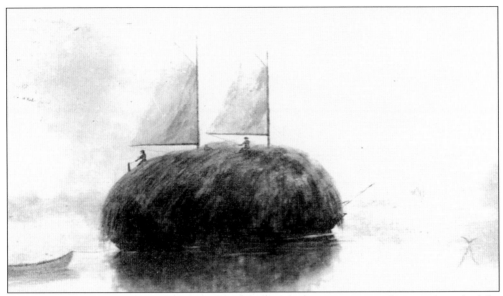

A salt hay scow is heaping with freshly harvested cordgrass *c.* 1911. Used primarily as feed for cattle, the grass was also used for mattress stuffing, insulation, and as packing material for fine china and other breakables.

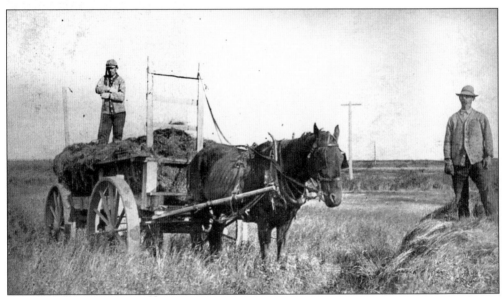

In this view, men harvest the salt hay at Beach Haven from the coastal marshes with a horse-drawn wagon. Both seaweed and salt hay were valuable and renewable resources of the island.

Two

THE LIGHTHOUSE
AND LIFESAVING

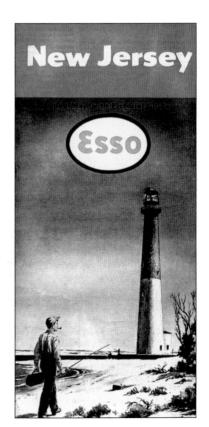

A 1951 Esso (Standard Oil Company of New Jersey) road map portrays a simple view of an angler off for a day of fishing near the famous Barnegat Lighthouse. This familiar red-and-white landmark has stood the test of time and today is a popular symbol of both the island and the surrounding area.

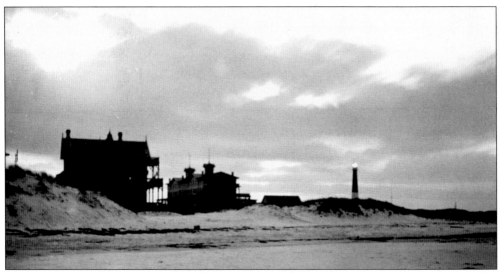

The Barnegat Light glows in the distance. The old wooden Oceanic Hotel can be seen in the center. This image dates from *c.* 1910.

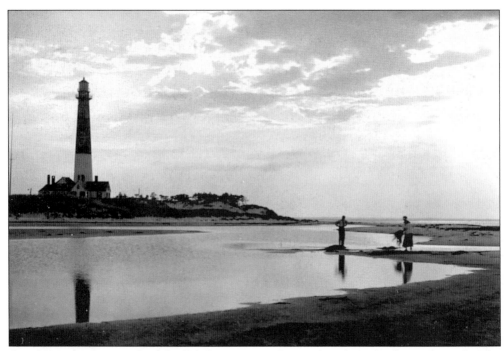

Another early photograph of the lighthouse is seen here, taken from the flats at low tide. The lighthouse keeper's house is seen standing next to the light at its base.

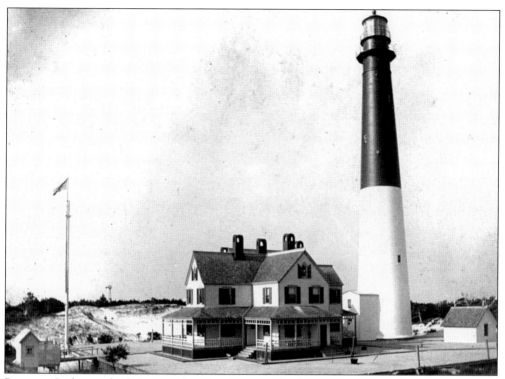

Barnegat Light was built in 1858 by Gen. George Meade to protect ships from the dangerous coastal waters. Later, in 1889, the keeper's house, a 20-room Victorian cottage, was built to provide housing for the lighthouse keepers and their families.

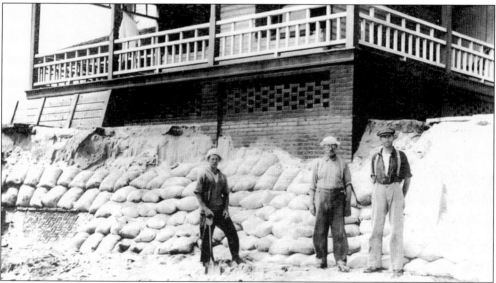

The lighthouse withstood many a great northeaster and is seen here shortly after a storm. Sandbags have been placed at the base of the keeper's house to protect it from dangerous winds and water. Erosion has been an ongoing problem for Long Beach Island for many years and was no different back then. Lighthouse keeper Clarence H. Cranmer is shown at the center of this photograph with two unidentified men.

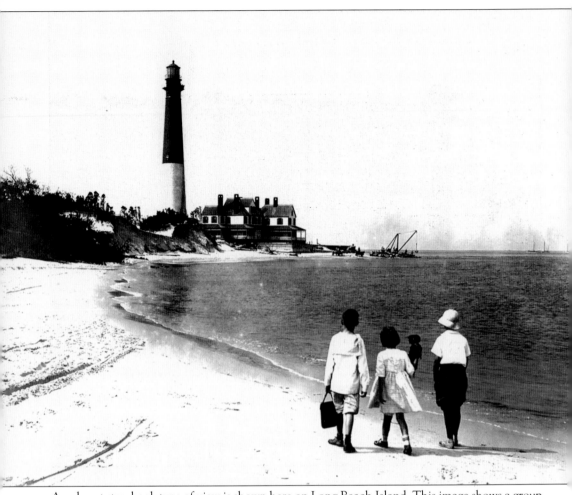

An almost storybook type of view is shown here on Long Beach Island. This image shows a group of children walking along the water's edge toward "Old Barney," as it was commonly called.

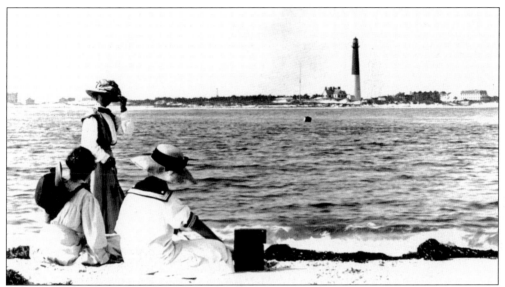

Three young people enjoy a day at the beach, with the lighthouse in the distance. Barnegat Light was and is a recognizable landmark for all those who have ever visited the Jersey Shore.

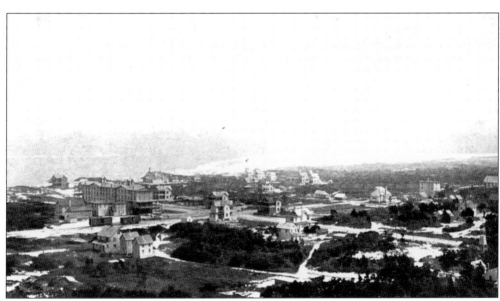

This is the view that you might have seen if you climbed the light *c.* 1910. There were many acres of undeveloped land for as far as you could see. The Oceanic Hotel is visible on the left.

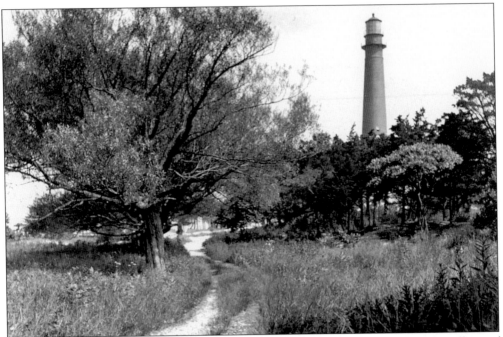

The immediate area around the lighthouse was originally quite wooded, but the effects of erosion and development later changed this natural-looking landscape.

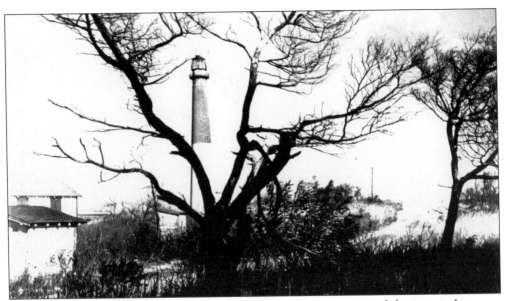

In another c. 1910 view, a better impression of the lush vegetation and dune grass that once surrounded the lighthouse and its outbuildings is apparent.

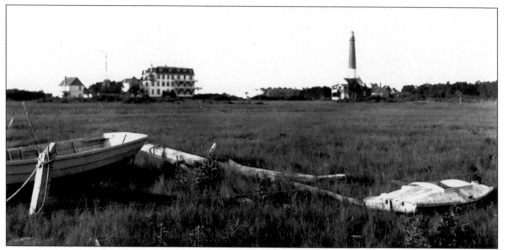

Pictured here is a tranquil scene of the meadows surrounding Barnegat Light (then called Barnegat City). To the left is the Sunset Hotel. Old wooden boats and a Barnegat Bay sneakbox can be seen in the foreground.

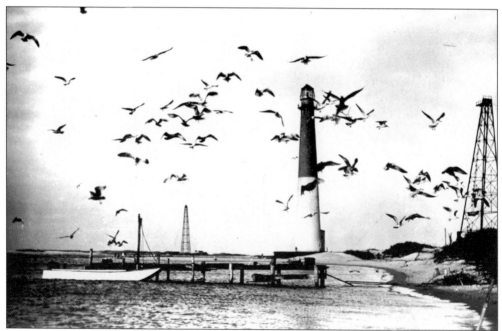

This much later view of historic Barnegat Lighthouse was probably taken in the 1940s. The town would be known as Barnegat City until 1948, when it officially changed its name to Barnegat Light.

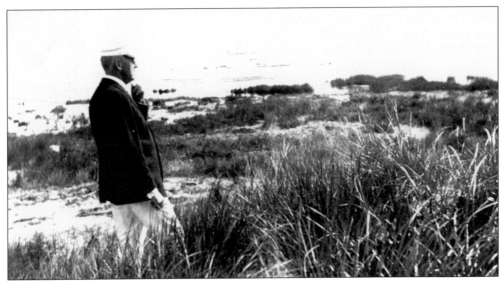

The many major storms that hit Long Beach Island through its history caused much destruction. The February 1920 storm would destroy the lighthouse keeper's house as well as the old Oceanic Hotel. The storms would also reshape the island itself and its shores. Inlets would close and reopen. In this view, the old inlet reopens on July 26, 1920.

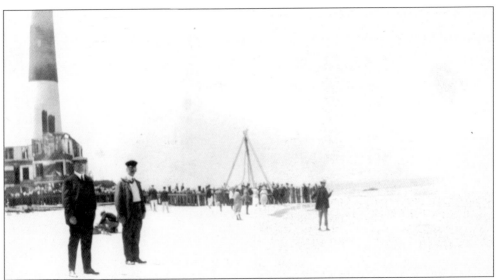

Jetties were constructed to help tame the elements and to control erosion. The lighthouse itself was once at risk. In this c. 1920 photograph, people gather on the beach to view the effects of the newly built jetty on the shoreline.

A celebration was held in 1957 to honor Gen. George Meade and the 100th anniversary of the Barnegat Light.

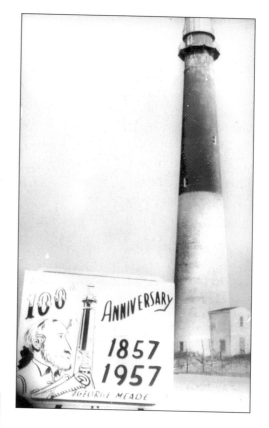

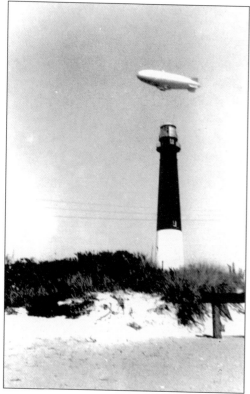

An unidentified blimp passes over the familiar red-and-white lighthouse in an image taken c. 1952. Blimps were often seen over the island and were used as submarine spotters during wartimes.

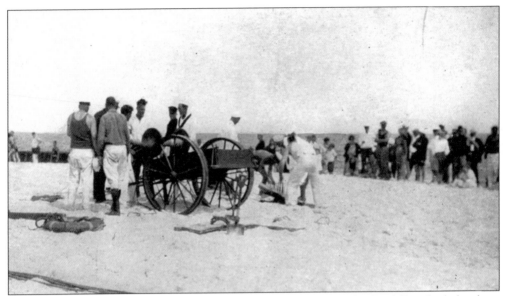

The lighthouse helped save many a ship off the coast of Long Beach Island. But the light alone could not save the many mariners shipwrecked off the coast. Local residents would do what they could to assist with rescues, but it was not until 1871 that the first lifesaving station was built on the Jersey Shore at Sandy Hook.

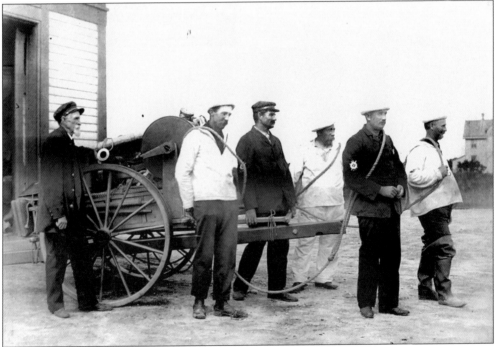

In 1872, lifesaving stations were built on Long Beach Island as well. Men were trained in all forms of rescue and became the lifeline for the imperiled. Lifesaving carts such as this were loaded with equipment and pulled to the water's edge during exercises and during actual emergencies. This crew is from Barnegat City c. the 1880s. Shown in the image are T. Birdsall, Loone Predmore, B. Ridgway, Joel Ridgway, C. Thompson, and B. Falkinburg.

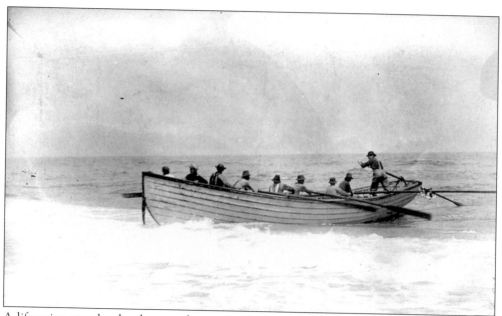

A lifesaving crew battles the pounding surf off LBI in this image. Surf boats were necessary to row out to ships wrecked on the shoals.

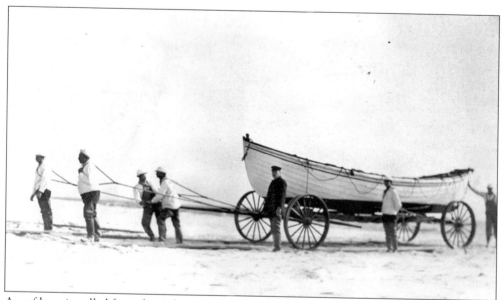

A surf boat is pulled from the Atlantic and loaded onto a cart. Men and sometimes horses were used to pull the heavy equipment up the sandy beach to the lifesaving station for storage.

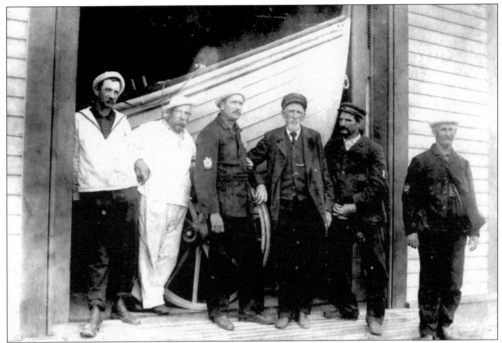

The crew of the Barnegat City station takes a moment out to pose for the camera. A typical surf boat can be seen in the station doorway.

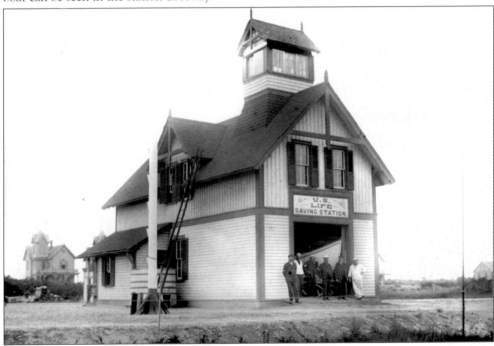

The Barnegat City lifesaving station is pictured here c. 1880. These two-story, cedar-shake buildings contained housing in the loft for the crew, a messroom for cooking and dining, and a boat room for equipment storage. A watchman could scan the horizon from the tall tower located above the station.

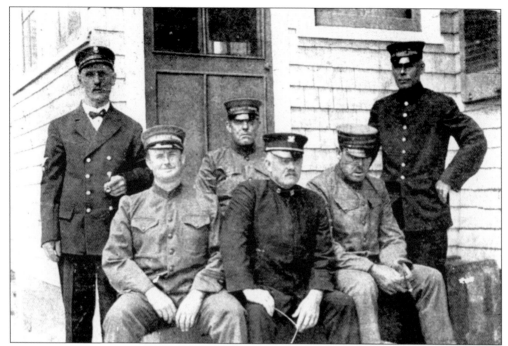

A crew of the Ship Bottom station poses c. 1917. The position of lifesaver was a well-respected occupation, with wages being paid of up to $40 a month.

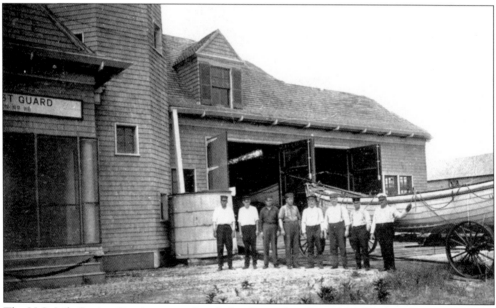

The U.S. Life-Saving Service merged with the Coast Guard in 1915. They took over operation of the old stations at Barnegat City, Loveladies, Harvey Cedars, Ship Bottom, Beach Haven Terrace, and Holgate (Bond's Station). There was also a station at Tucker's Island, which was abandoned in 1932. The station shown here is from Ship Bottom.

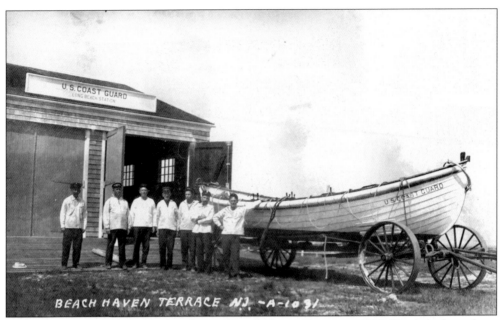

Proud surf men pose alongside their boat at Beach Haven Terrace *c.* 1922. The large barn doors on the station always faced southwest, allowing them to be opened easier during a northeaster.

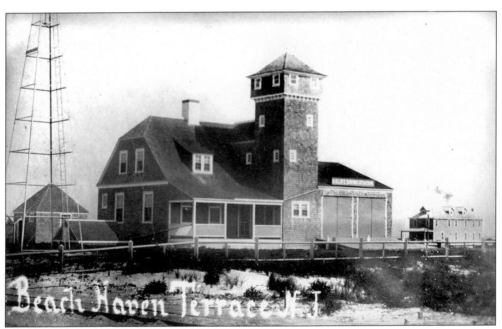

Built in 1902, the Beach Haven Terrace station is shown among the dunes. Known as red houses because of their universal reddish-brown paint, they were usually lettered and numbered with the station designation in bright white paint.

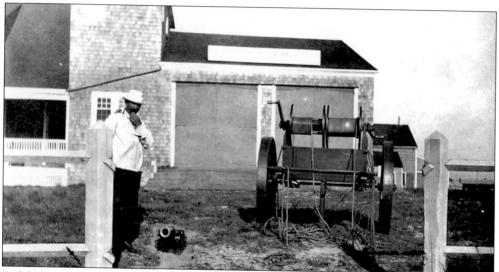

A lifesaver is shown with his shot line and surf gun at Beach Haven Terrace. A small cannonlike gun was used to propel a line from the shore to the nearby ship. A piece of rescue equipment called a breeches buoy could then be used to shuttle survivors to the safety of shore.

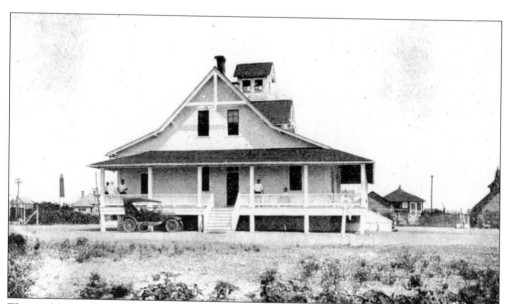

The usefulness of the old lifesaving stations, such as this one at Barnegat City, began to decline in the 1920s. The coming of the much safer steamships decreased the amount of shipwrecks offshore. The stations' focus shifted more toward beach patrol and to other offshore patrol duties.

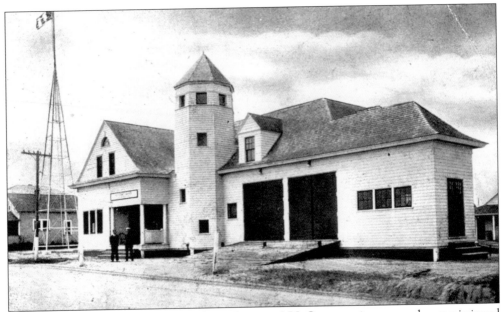

Another classic lifesaving station is shown here on LBI. Some stations once decommissioned were later reused as private homes or fishing clubs or for other purposes. But many were torn down, as was the case with the Ship Bottom station shown here.

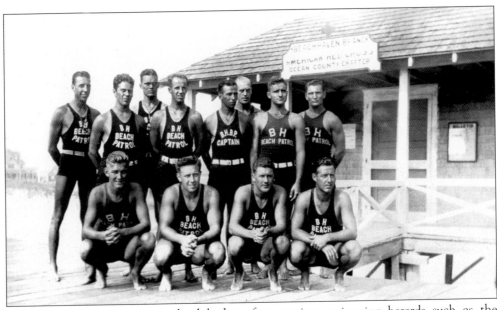

Lifeguards helped to protect island bathers from various swimming hazards such as the dangerous undertow and strong rip currents. The Beach Haven patrol poses for a group shot.

Three

SHIPWRECKS AND
THE *LUCY EVELYN*

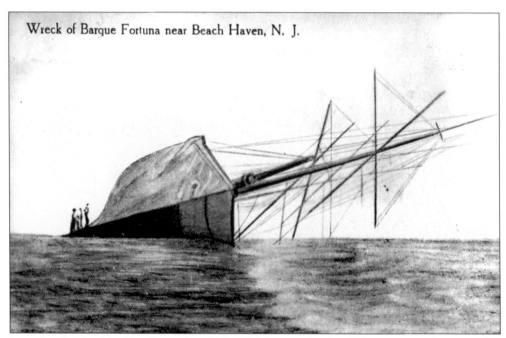

Wreck of Barque Fortuna near Beach Haven, N. J.

Long Beach Island had its share of tragic shipwrecks over the last 200 or so years. Its geographic location along shipping lanes, the lack of modern navigational tools aboard the ships, and naturally occurring adverse weather conditions often caused both large and small ships to wreck offshore.

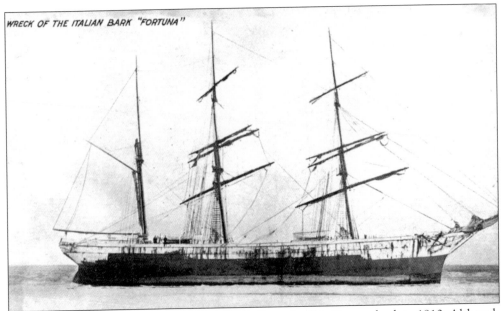

The Italian bark *Fortuna* came aground off 16th Street in Ship Bottom back in 1910. Although the ship itself was lost, all of the passengers were saved, including a newborn baby, a pig, and a cat. If not for the lifesaving service and its equipment, all may have been lost.

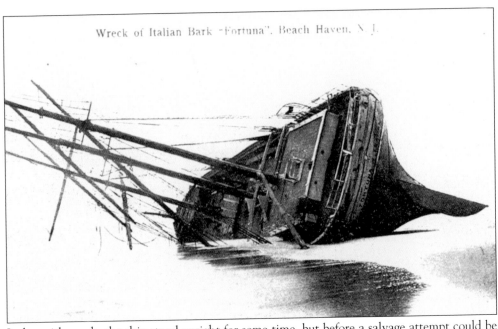

Wreck of Italian Bark "Fortuna". Beach Haven, N. J.

Laden with goods, the ship stood upright for some time, but before a salvage attempt could be made, the waves rolled the massive ship onto its side. Locals as well as tourists flocked to the beach to see the wreck.

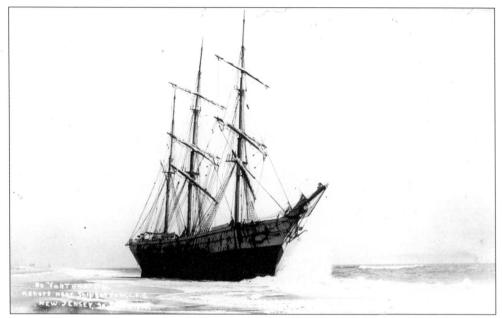

Included here is another image of the tall-masted ship *Fortuna* just before the vessel succumbed to the heavy surf. Photographs such as these conjure up images of pirates and buried treasure along the coast.

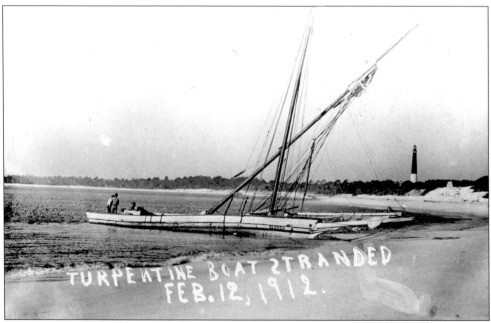

Here, a much smaller ship, called a turpentine boat, is beached near the lighthouse in Barnegat City on February 12, 1912. Note the backward letters on the postcard description. This was a frequent occurrence since many of these photographs were labeled by writing the title of the image backward directly on the negative, through a small window on the back of the box camera being used.

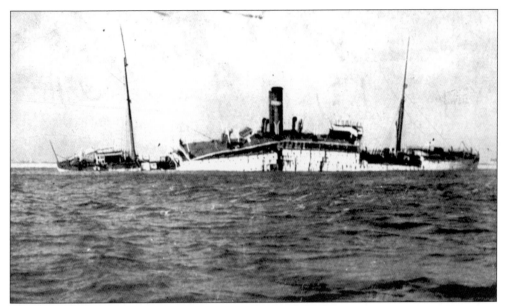

This U.S. Army transport ship, the *Sumner,* was lost on December 12, 1916. It came onto the shoals about a mile offshore, just south of the Barnegat Inlet. As was often the case, dense fog was the reported cause of the accident.

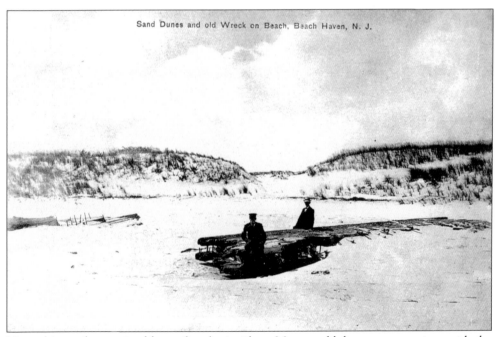

Many shipwrecks remained long after the incident. Most would disappear over time, with the tides washing away the bulk of the damaged ship, and the rest being covered beneath the sands. Here, only a few broken spars of the ship remain.

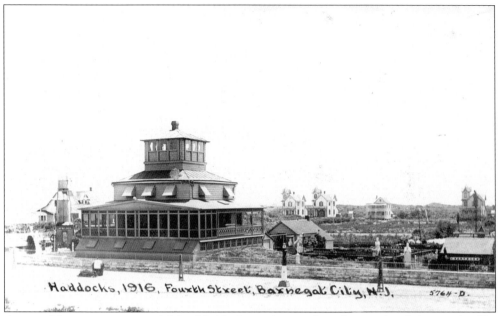

Haddocks, 1916, Fourth Street, Barnegat City, N.J.   5764-D.

A retired businessman named John Haddock was known for salvaging local shipwrecks. His house, on Fourth Street in Barnegat City, was adorned with his finds from the various ships wrecked on the local beaches. Anchors, ship nameplates, beautiful carved figureheads, ship wheels, lamps, and even a whole pilothouse could have been found proudly displayed on his property shown here. His house was moved back away from the ocean several times to avoid destruction by the sea.

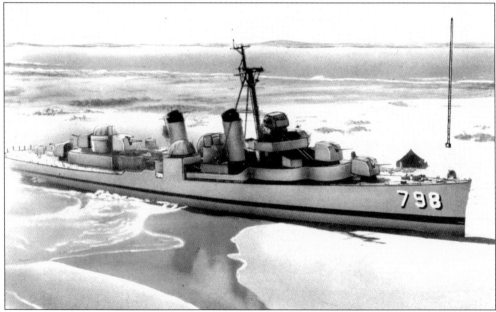

Modern-day shipwrecks along the Jersey Shore are somewhat uncommon. On March 6, 1962, however, the U.S. Navy destroyer *Monssen* ran aground at Holgate. Driven by high tides and strong gale winds, it remained onshore for over a month before navy salvage crews could remove it.

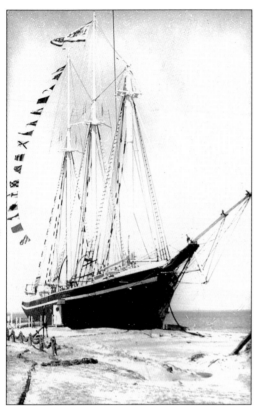

The *Lucy Evelyn*, built in 1917, sailed worldwide carrying such cargo as lumber, coal, and tobacco. In 1948, it was purchased and brought to its new home in Beach Haven to be used as a tourist attraction and gift shop.

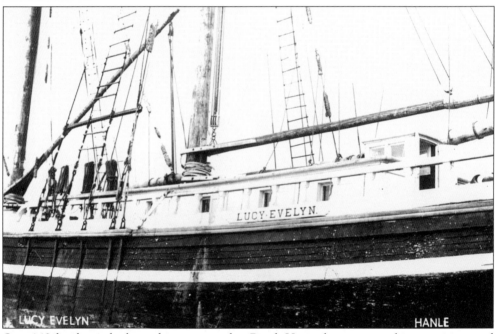

Over 140 feet long, the large ship was towed to Beach Haven by tug, moved into position, and dredged into dry land. The ship was in remarkable shape for its age. An informative maritime history display was created onboard, and a retail shop space was created.

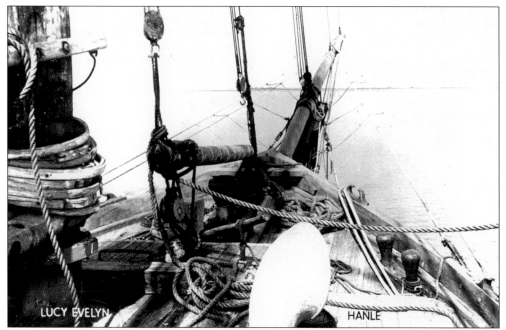

Shown here is a scene aboard the *Lucy Evelyn* near the bow. With all its original hardware and rigging in place, it seemed as if the boat could set sail at a moment's notice.

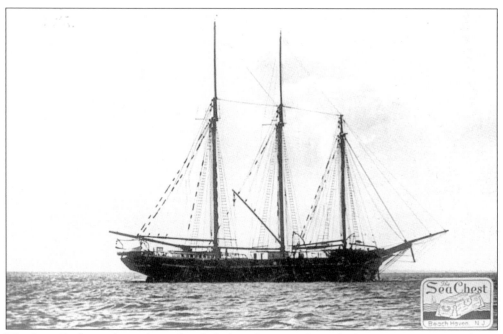

The *Lucy Evelyn* is shown here shortly before the move from the bay to its permanent home on shore.

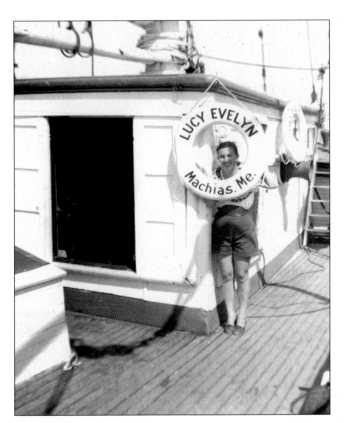

This candid snapshot of the author's mother, Yolanda Hartnett, was taken aboard the *Lucy Evelyn* c. 1949.

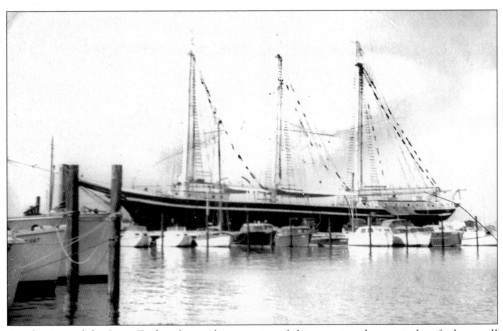

A side view of the *Lucy Evelyn* shows the true size of this massive ship as it dwarfs the small pleasure boats docked nearby. This photograph was taken in 1953.

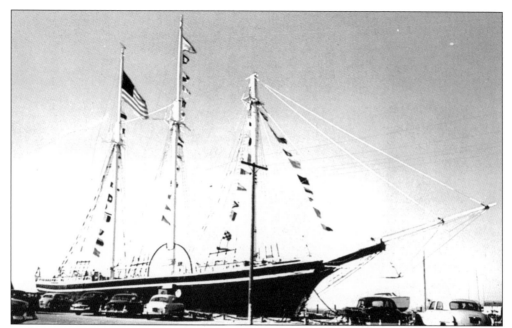

A favorite destination for visiting tourists, the *Lucy Evelyn* was a familiar sight with its multicolored flags waving in the breeze.

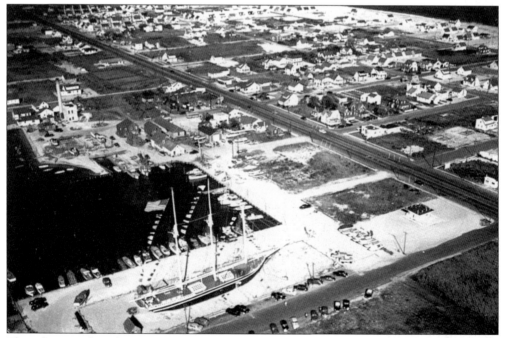

This photograph, taken from the air, better shows the position of the ship on land. The property around the *Lucy Evelyn* was quite vacant back then and later became prime seashore building lots.

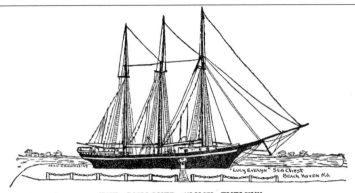

THE SCHOONER "LUCY EVELYN"

Built in 1917, Harrington, Maine, by Captain E. C. Lindsey, Machias, Me.
Launched Thanksgiving Day & named for his two daughters Lucy & Evelyn.
Original cost of building $64,000, today probably about $200,000.
Registered length 140 feet, beam 32 feet, draft 10 feet, net tonnage 307.
Outside planking 4″ pine, ribs 8″ x 8″, ceiling 8″ x 12″, deck 3½″ spruce.
Masts, booms and gaffs are Oregon pine, Knees are Maine Hackmatack.
Speed loaded about ten knots, New York to Norfolk just five days.
No Auxiliary power, electricity, radio nor refrigeration.
Only power 15 H. P. donkey engine in forcastle to raise anchor & sails.
Cargoes: lumber, coal, rock, gypsum, potatoes, molasses, tobacco & salt.
Ports: Machiasport, New York, Philadelphia, Charleston, Mobile, Savannah, Nova Scotia, Puerto Rico, Virgin Islands, Barbados, Cape Verde and Liverpool.
Five man crew: Captain, Steward, Mate and two Seamen.
Operated by Captain Lindsey 1917 to 1940, Lucy Evelyn Inc. 1940 to 1944, Captain John Costa, New Bedford 1944 to 1948, The Sea Chest - - - - 1948.
Sunk Twice: Martha's Vyd., Rock Jetty 1942, Cape Cod, seam opened 1938.
We bought her at auction $1550 New Bedford, June 9, 1948 – towed to Beach Haven by tug. During October 7, 1948 high tide moved her to present spot, dredged her into dry land, filled sand around her and raised her 4 feet.

Please respect and help us preserve this fine example of an old sailing ship, so that future generations may be able to enjoy it.

We would appreciate any information regarding items of historic interest concerning the sailing era of the past that would fit into our Marine Museum on deck.

THANK YOU

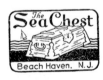

GIFTS   SPORTING GOODS

BEACH HAVEN, N. J.   BETTY & NAT EWER

Here is an original promotional leaflet describing the *Lucy Evelyn*. Sadly, the ship was destroyed in a horrific fire in February 1972. All attempts to save the landmark were unsuccessful.

Four
BEACH AND BOARDWALK

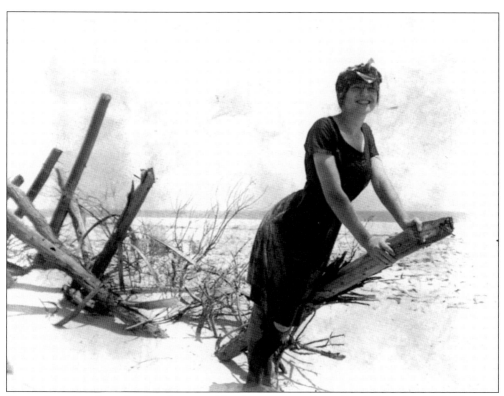

Shown here is a classic bathing beauty of the day posing on Long Beach Island c. 1917. Florence Bernard Hartnett (the grandmother of the author) is pictured at Harvey Cedars, posing among the dunes and driftwood.

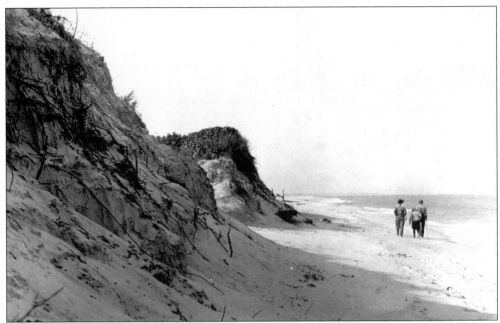

The beaches of LBI have always lured visitors with their warm sands, natural beauty, and melodic crashing of waves. The dunes were larger back then, before the erosion and development took its toll.

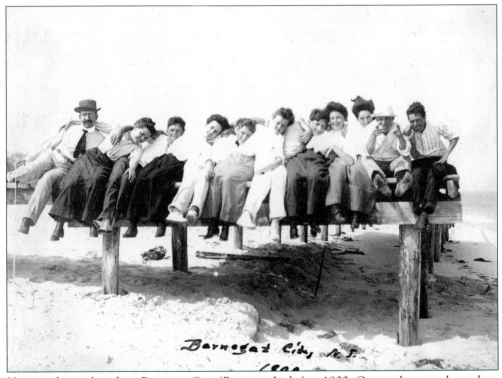

Here is a happy bunch at Barnegat City (Barnegat Light) *c*. 1900. Group photographs such as these were popular keepsakes of trips to LBI.

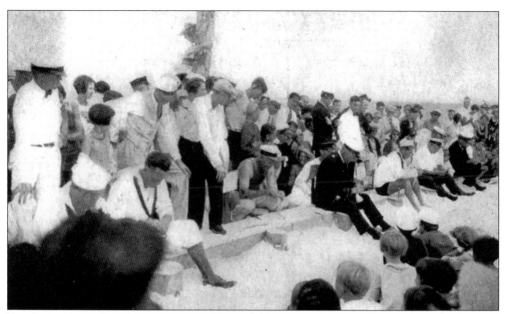

Beaches were not for just sunning oneself. Beachfront contests were a fun pastime. Here, several men compete in a knot-tying contest at High Point *c*. 1910.

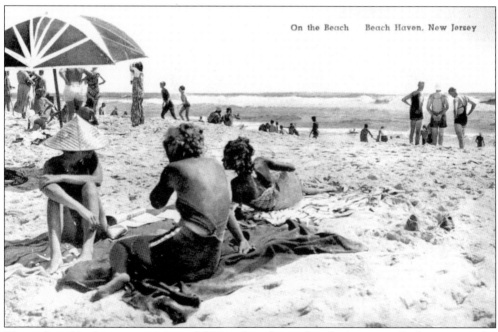

On the Beach   Beach Haven, New Jersey

The styles of bathing suits seen on LBI beaches changed with the times. Bathing suit styles developed from one-piece woolen suits for both men and women to more daring ones, as seen in this 1940s image.

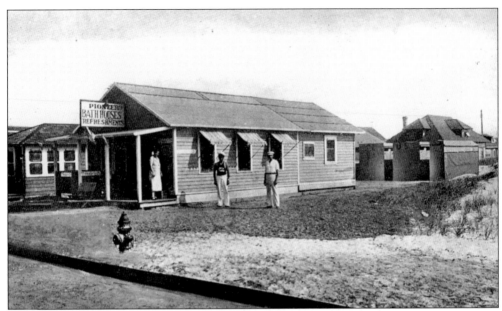

Bathhouses were located up and down the island. This is the Pioneer Bath House, located at 21st Street in Beach Arlington (Ship Bottom).

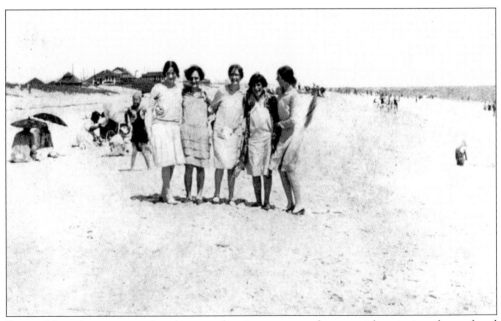

Pictured here is a common beach scene showing a group of young girls enjoying the surf and sand in Ship Bottom c. 1931.

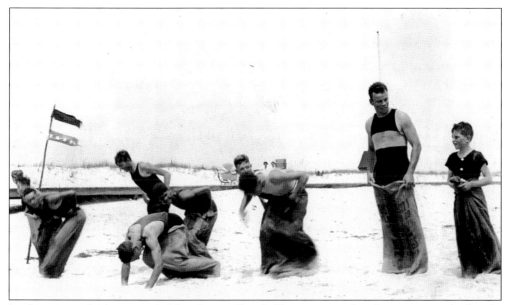

In this view, which was probably taken at Beach Haven, is another fun event on the beach. Games such as these were usually held on special occasions.

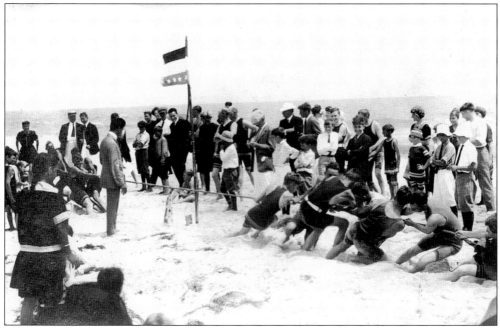

Here is the classic tug of war match, shown at Beach Haven c. 1913. Cards such as these could have been taken by anyone with an early box camera and brought to a nearby photographer for processing into prints or picture postcards. This one was developed and printed by Louis P. Selden, a Beach Haven photographer.

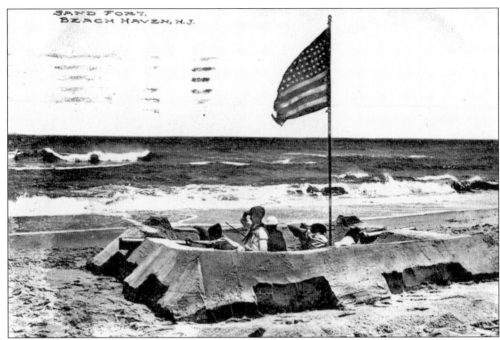

SAND FORT,
BEACH HAVEN, N.J.

Remember building sandcastles and sand forts on the beach? This is the ultimate in sand sculpture, complete with cannons and an American flag. This photograph was taken *c.* 1914.

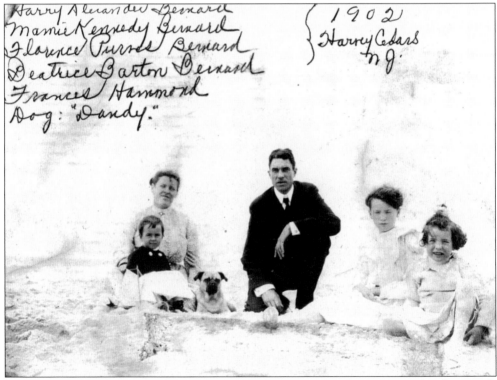

Harry Alexander Bernard
Mamie Kennedy Bernard
Florence Purves Bernard
Beatrice Barton Bernard
Frances Hammond
Dog: "Dandy."

1902
Harvey Cedars
N.J.

The Bernard family and their dog pose on the beach at Harvey Cedars in 1902. The photograph includes the grandmother and the great-grandparents of author George C. Hartnett.

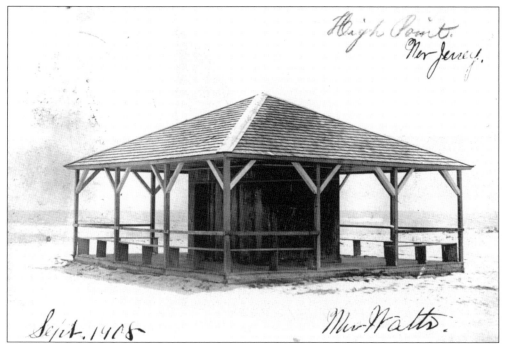

This is a typical Jersey-style bathhouse pavilion at High Point, Long Beach Island. Such structures provided changing rooms and a respite from the sun.

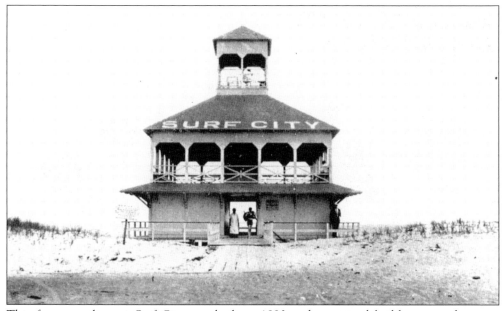

This fancy pavilion at Surf City was built *c.* 1890 and contained bathhouses and storage facilities for township equipment. It was destroyed by the great hurricane of 1944.

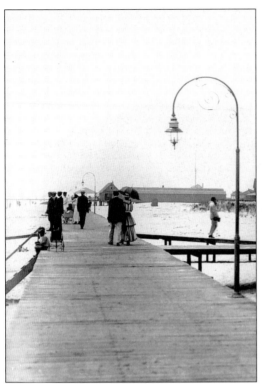

An early wooden boardwalk was constructed at Beach Haven in 1898. It consisted of wood planks laid over the beach sand. It was replaced in 1916 by a bigger and better boardwalk, covering over 22 blocks in length.

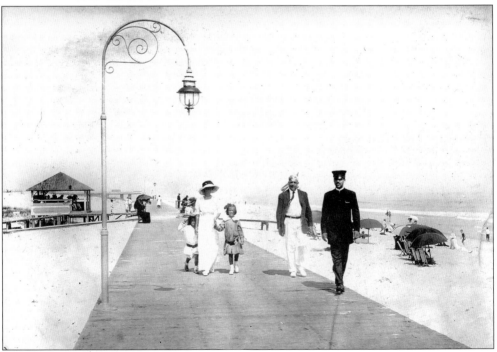

The new boardwalk was the place to be seen in Beach Haven. Finely dressed families, men in suits, and women with parasols strolled along, taking in the sights and sounds of the ocean. At night, the boardwalk was illuminated by the ornate gas lamps shown here.

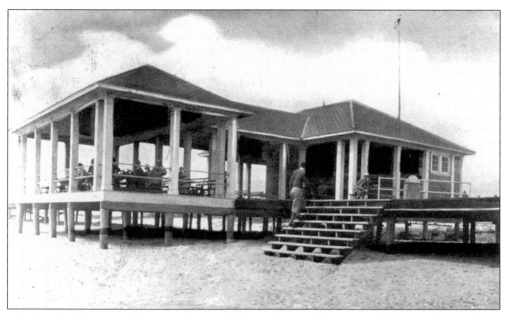

The boardwalk at Beach Haven also included a fine pavilion, perfect for providing a shady retreat from the sun.

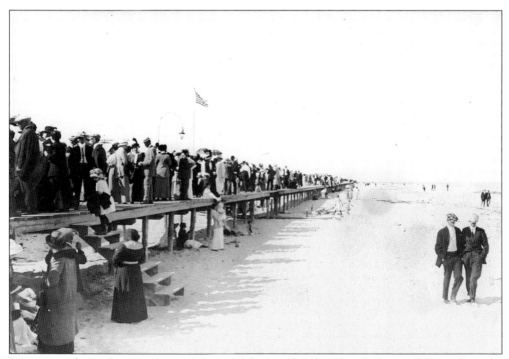

This image shows the immense popularity of the boardwalk at Beach Haven. Scores of people, dressed in their finest, stroll the walkway. This may have been the day of some type of special event or celebration. Note the lack of any railings or handrails along the boardwalk span.

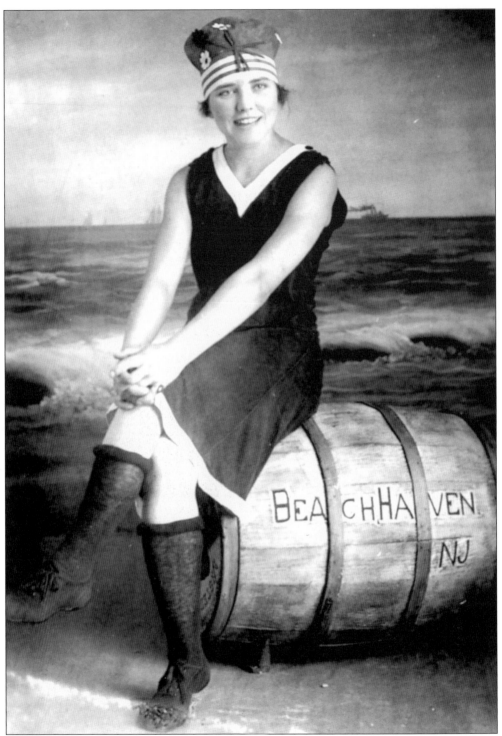

Studio shots taken in front of a painted backdrop were popular souvenirs. Here, a young lady poses in her period bathing attire while sitting on a barrel labeled "Beach Haven NJ." Paper moon themes were also a popular alternative.

Five

HOTELS AND LODGING

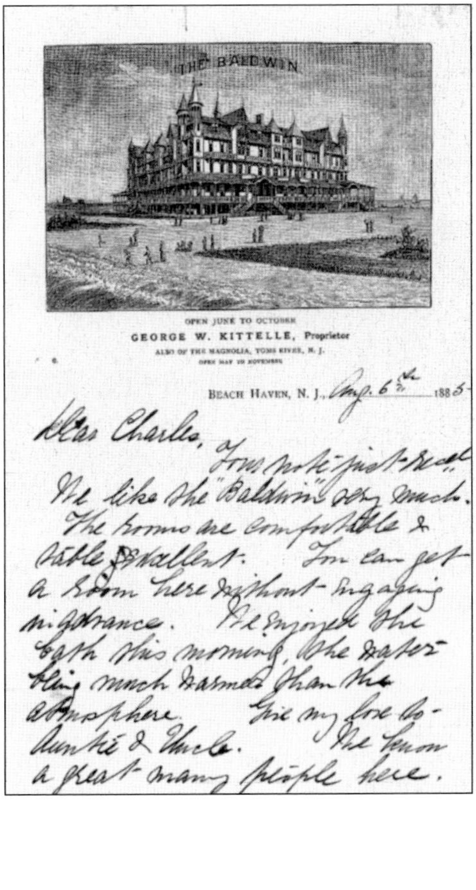

Long Beach Island was home to many types of lodging, from small rooming houses to cottages to lavish hotels. Pictured here is a sheet of early hotel stationery advertising the Hotel Baldwin c. 1885.

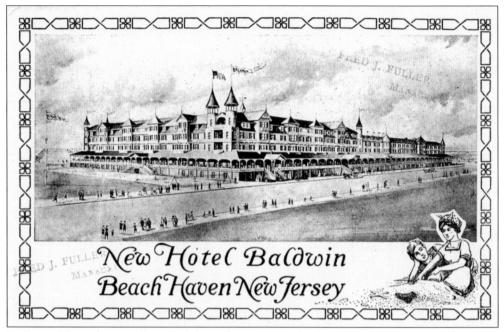

Built in 1883 and originally called the Arlington Inn, the hotel was later renamed the Hotel Baldwin. Named after Matthias Baldwin, a builder of steam locomotives, the hotel greatly resembled a storybook castle.

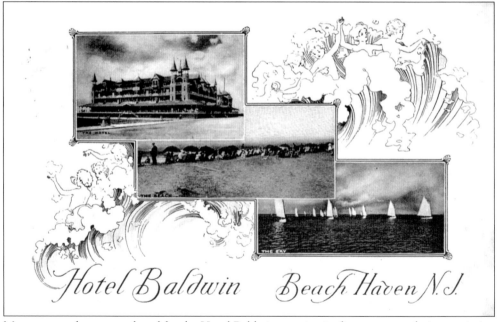

Many postcards were produced for the Hotel Baldwin, touting its fine accommodations, pristine beaches, and healthy setting. Guests arrived at the hotel via horse-drawn railway cars up to c. 1896.

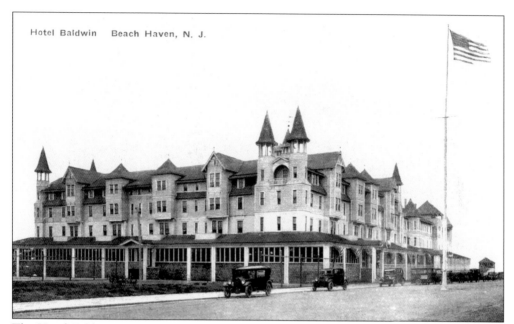

The Hotel Baldwin contained several bars, two bowling alleys, and a billiard room. Gunning and trap shooting contests were part of their regular events for hotel guests, as well as ballroom dances, parties, and other social events.

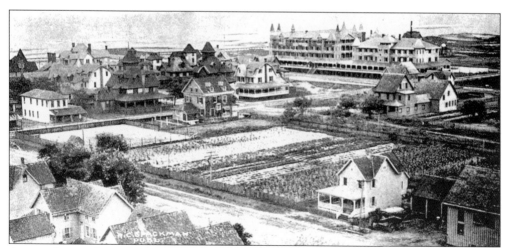

An aerial view shows the large Hotel Baldwin in the distance. Around the hotel were several large parcels of land that produced garden-fresh vegetables and fresh flowers for display throughout the hotel.

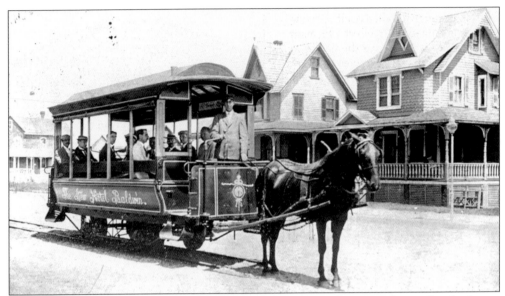

Pictured here is the Hotel Baldwin horse-drawn trolley at Beach Haven. Ironically, the horses replaced an earlier 1884 steam locomotive, which did not fare well in the salty ocean air.

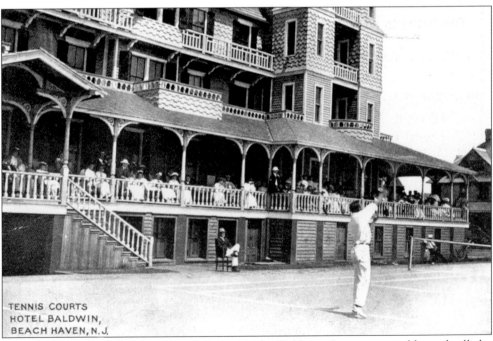

TENNIS COURTS
HOTEL BALDWIN,
BEACH HAVEN, N.J.

A first-class tennis facility was found on-site at the Baldwin. Spectators could watch all the action from the wide porches and balconies of the hotel while enjoying a cool drink and ocean breezes.

The Hotel Baldwin billed itself as "New Jersey's leading summer resort." Its main competition for guests was the nearby Engleside Hotel, which catered to a more family-oriented crowd.

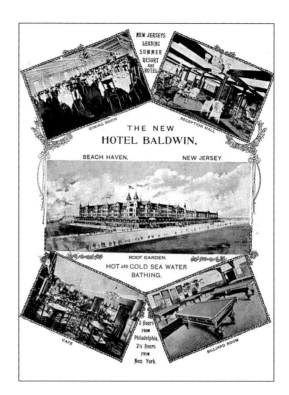

The Baldwin Locomotive Works

NAME _Dreage Fred_

SHOP _____

REGISTER NO. _3 4r-190_

NOTICE TO EMPLOYEES

You must report your time daily to your Foreman or Clerk, also to the Office Timekeeper; otherwise your time will not be entered upon the pay roll.

You will be paid on Friday evening of each week after the signal to quit work is given.

You must get in line on pay day according to number.

As you pass your foreman in line call your NUMBER to him and your NAME at the pay window.

If you are sent from the shops to do work on the firm's account and desire your family to draw your

(over)

Included here is an employee identification card from a worker at the Baldwin Locomotive Works in Pennsylvania. Matthias Baldwin was the principal financier of the Hotel Baldwin and its namesake.

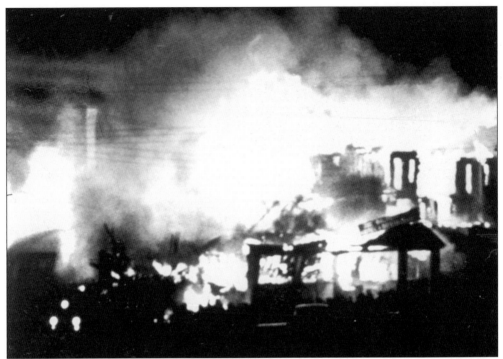

On the evening of September 24, 1960, a fire broke out in an empty wing of the Hotel Baldwin. Driven by gale-force winds that night, the fire engulfed the old wooden hotel in a spectacular blaze. Over 20 local fire companies from as far away as Toms River would battle the blaze, but the historic structure could not be saved.

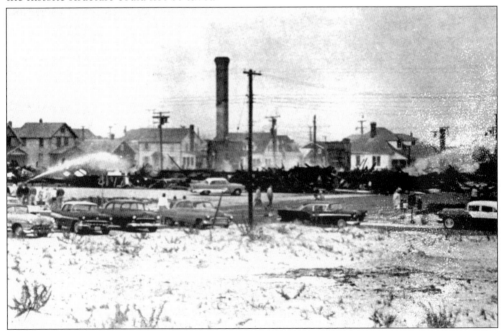

The hotel was a total loss and was never rebuilt. The debris was eventually cleaned up, and a church was later built on the site.

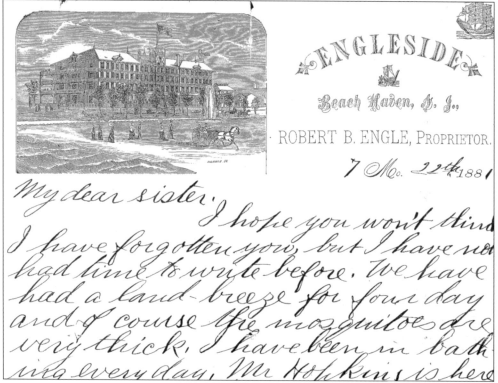

My dear sister, I hope you won't think I have forgotten you, but I have not had time to write before. We have had a land-breeze for four day and of course the mosquitoes are very thick. I have been in bathing every day. Mr Hopkins is here

In 1876, a large wooden hotel was built at South and Amber Streets in Beach Haven. Robert Engle, a Quaker from Mount Holly, set out to build a hotel of unequal status. A letter written on hotel stationery from 1881 reads, "We have had a land breeze for a day and of course the mosquitoes are very thick."

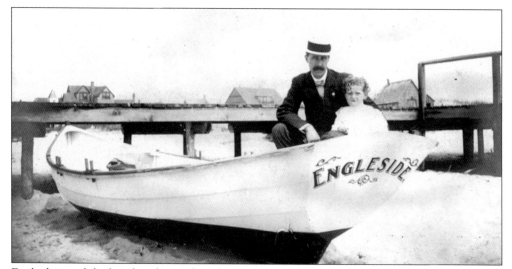

Engle designed the hotel so that each and every room had an ocean view. It also had both sea and fresh water available for bathing. The hotel's many amenities attracted the upper-middle class from Philadelphia. Here, John and Emma Good pose in one of the Engleside Hotel rowboats.

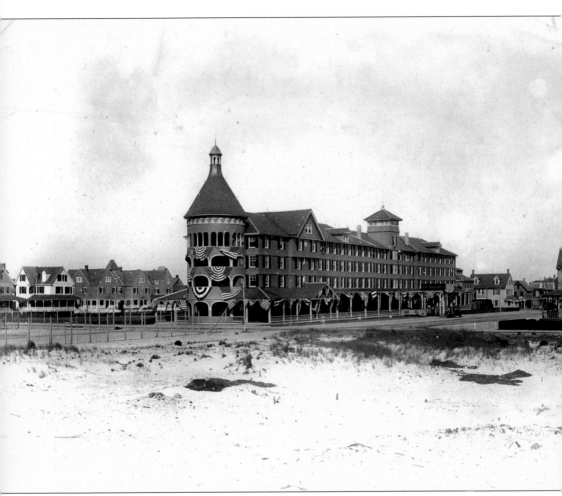

Built at right angles to the ocean, rooms had both cool breezes and spectacular views. Over 300 rooms were often filled to capacity, and most visitors normally stayed for months at a time. Suites of rooms were also available for larger families and their service staff. Babies could drink fresh milk straight from the three Guernsey cows maintained by the hotel. Servers in crisp, starched uniforms served hotel patrons in fancy dining rooms. The Engleside prided itself on its temperance policy, allowing no liquor within its hotel. Visitors desiring such evils would have to frequent the nearby Hotel Baldwin.

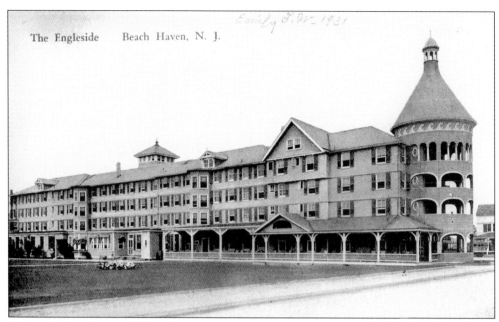

The Engleside   Beach Haven, N. J.   *Emily F. Mc 1931*

Robert Engle, who would later become a state senator, was very proud of his lavish hotel and prided himself on the special attention given to every guest. He died in 1901, but his tradition was carried on by his son, Robert F. Engle.

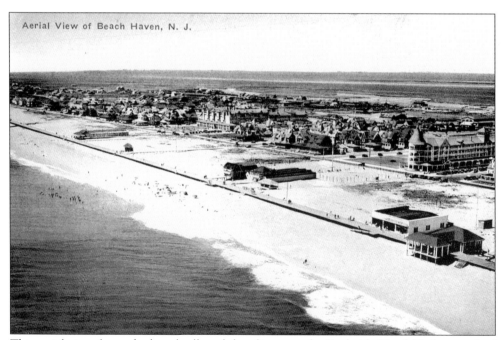

Aerial View of Beach Haven, N. J.

This aerial view shows the boardwalk and shoreline near the Engleside Hotel. Today, much of this same area is occupied by large oceanfront homes.

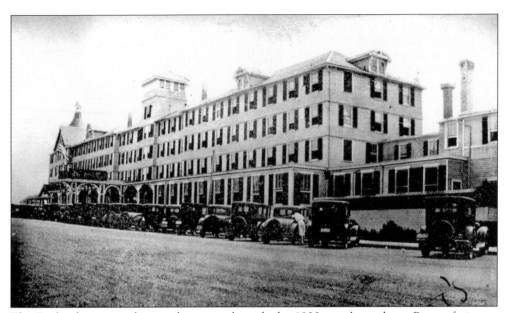

The Engleside remained a popular resort through the 1930s, as shown here. Rows of vintage automobiles line the streets around this popular hotel.

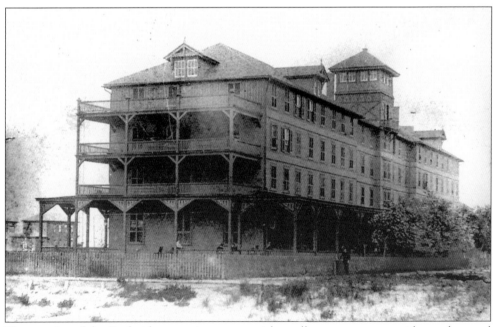

The exterior of the Engleside was quite ornate, with a tall tower at center, wide porches, and spacious balconies. This photograph was probably taken c. 1880.

Tennis was also a passion of Robert Engle, and he built a fine set of tennis club courts at his grand hotel. Women and men could enjoy the sport on hard dirt courts built alongside the hotel. Famous tennis stars of the day often came to the hotel to play popular exhibition matches.

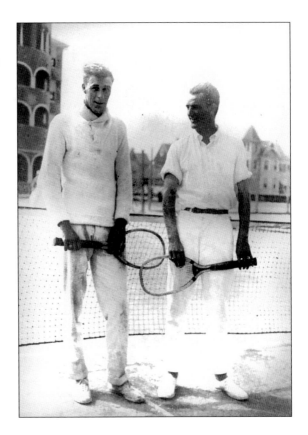

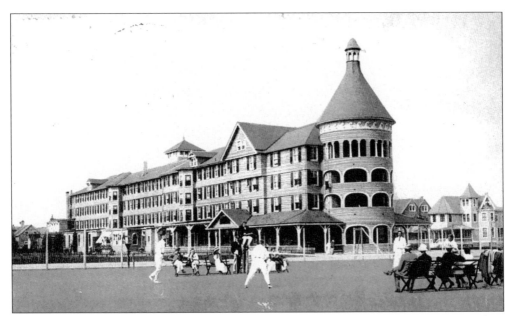

Pictured here is a nice view of the Engleside Hotel, with its turret-shaped tower at one end. A group of people has come out for a tennis match at one of the hotel's dirt courts.

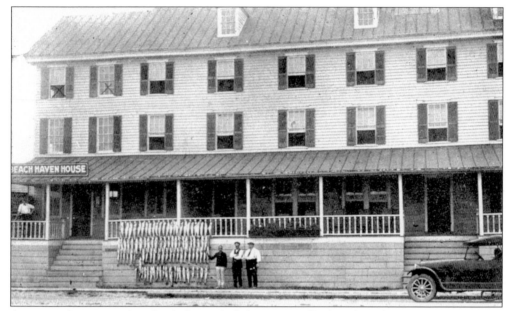

Accommodations on the island also included many smaller hotels such as this one in Beach Haven. The Beach Haven House was built in 1874, and rooms could be had for $12 a week, a somewhat large sum back in the day. Indoor plumbing was added to the hotel in 1895 to serve its 65 guest rooms.

Beach Haven House,

Beach Haven, = = = = = New Jersey.

MRS. JULIA MULHOLLAND.

Delightful Summer Resort.   Bay and Ocean View.   Good Fishing, Sailing or Bathing.

....189

Mr & Mrs. H. A. Bernard Dr.
To Mrs Julia Mulholland.
For board one week at $12 00 per week
and two days
          Total one week $ 24 00
          two days   7 00
     Baggage   2 0
          Total $ 3 1 2 0
Received Payment
     Mrs Julia Mulholland
          July 11th 18/92

The Beach Haven House was originally run by Julia Mulholland. Many of the island's hotels were run by women. The hotel remained a popular place to stay up through the 1920s and became a speakeasy during Prohibition. The hotel was torn down c. 1967.

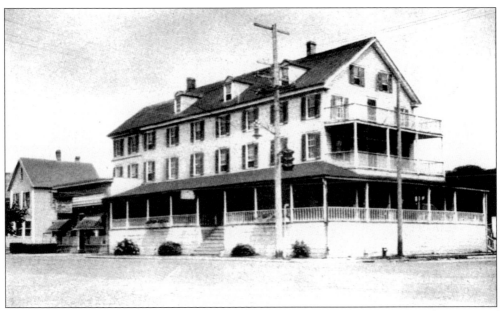

This image shows a much later view of the old Beach Haven House, located at the corner of Bay and Centre Streets in Beach Haven. In the 1950s, it was commonly known as Lambs, after its owner.

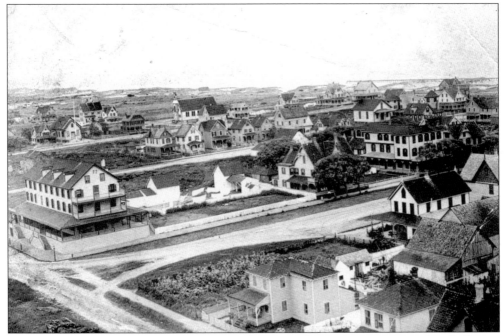

An early cabinet card image shows the area from a rooftop or water tower in Beach Haven. Visible on the left is the Beach Haven House on the corner, as well as many homes and small rooming houses.

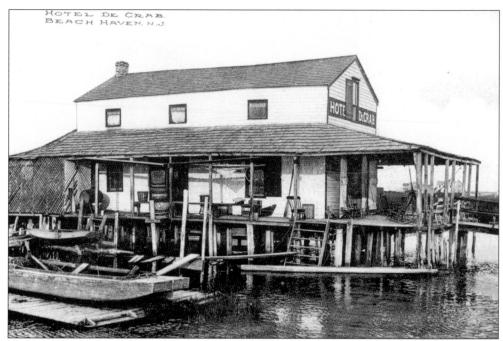

An interesting old hotel on Long Beach Island was called the Hotel DeCrab. It began its history in Harvey Cedars in 1847, but it was moved via barge to its new home here on Dock Road in Beach Haven c. 1873. Its clientele consisted of transient people, including local boat captains and those waiting for passenger service to the mainland.

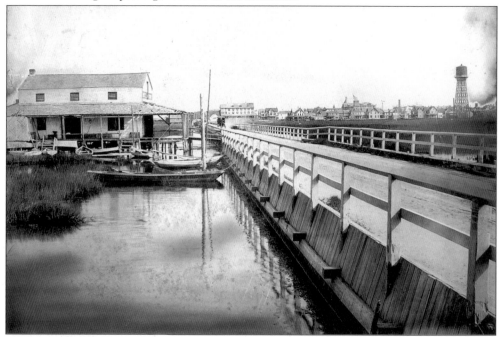

Built on piers, the Hotel DeCrab sat along rural Dock Road near the bay's edge. This early photograph was taken looking east toward the Beach Haven House (in the distance). The hotel, once the oldest building in Beach Haven, was torn down in 1984.

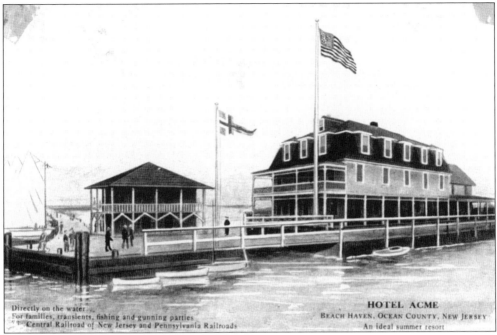

In 1904, a brand-new hotel was opened by John Cranmer in Beach Haven. Called the Hotel Acme, it stood on the water's edge at Dock Road. Known early on for its fishing and gunning parties, it would later become notorious for drinking during Prohibition.

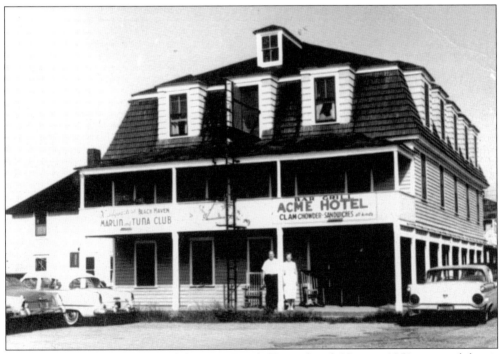

Seen here is a 1950s snapshot of the same Beach Haven hotel. Vintage 1950s automobiles sit out front, and a sign over the door welcomes the Beach Haven Marlin and Tuna Club.

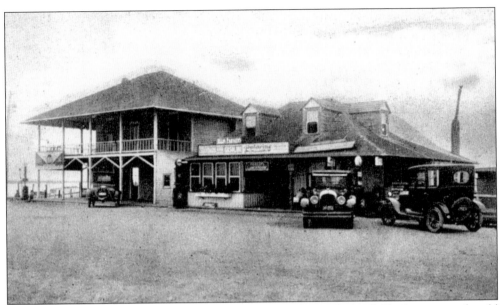

Next to the Beach Haven Yacht Club stood the old Public Dock Hotel. Easily seen are the old automobiles parked out front. Many smaller hotels such as this catered to the casual tourist and thrived during the busy holiday weeks.

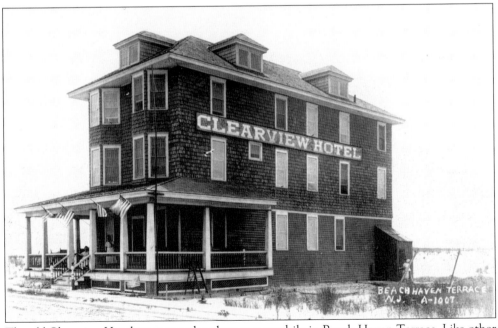

The old Clearview Hotel was a popular place to stay while in Beach Haven Terrace. Like other small hotels, it became a speakeasy during Prohibition, serving alcohol smuggled onto the island by small boats under the cover of darkness.

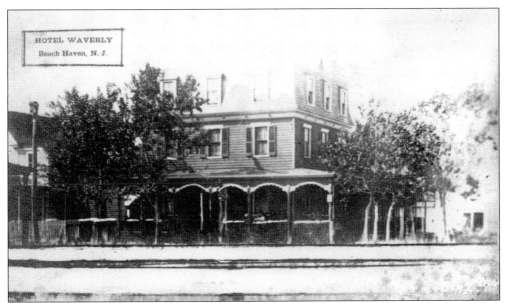

HOTEL WAVERLY
Beach Haven, N. J.

Looking back in the history of Long Beach Island, only the towns of Barnegat City and Beach Haven were purposely planned as true resort communities. But back in 1882, a small community was planned on the northern border of Beach Haven to rival the already established island resorts. Planned by an Englishman named William Hewitt, he built a hotel on-site called the Waverly House. But Hewitt's idea never gained acceptance by the general public, and his dream never resulted in more than the hotel shown here. Today, the area is developed and called North Beach Haven.

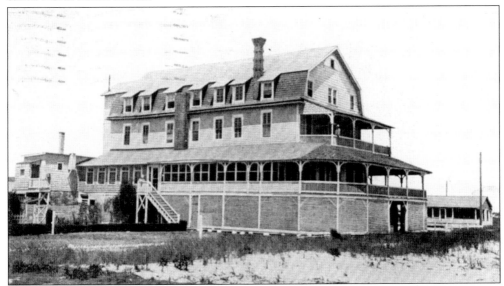

Located not far from the Hotel Waverly, between 13th and 14th Streets, was the Breakers Hotel. Built in 1886, it was originally called the Dolphin Inn. The owner William Ringgold sold the hotel in 1889 and moved farther north on the island to build a private home and establish a small community of cottages that his daughter named Spray Beach. His home was eventually converted into the Spray Beach Hotel. The Hotel Waverly was eventually lost to the 1944 hurricane.

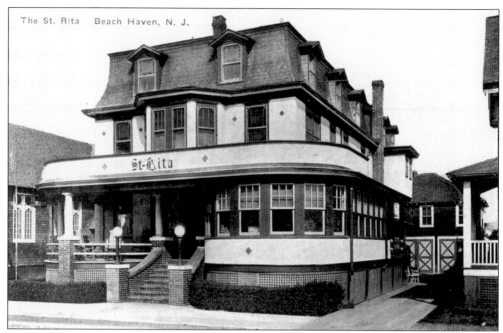

The St. Rita Hotel was located in Beach Haven. It was used during the 1940s as housing for the U.S. military, as were many of the smaller hotels.

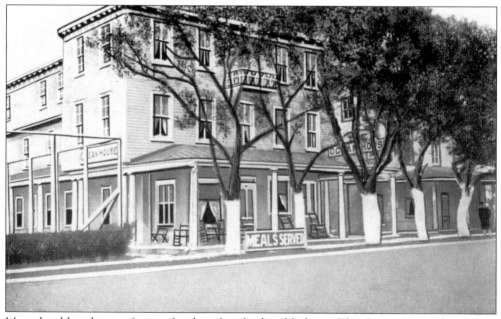

Many local hotels were famous for their fine food and lodging. The Ocean House, located on the north side of Center Street between Beach and Bay Avenues in Beach Haven, was no different. A sign displayed out front advertised "Meals Served."

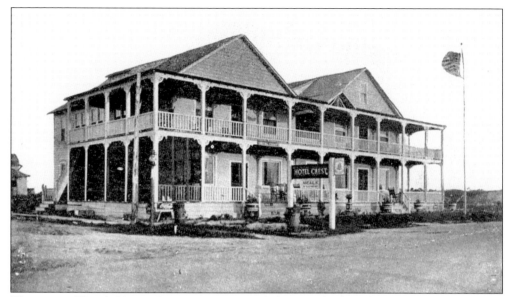

The town of Beach Haven Crest grew up around the pound fishing business that was thriving in the area at the time. The nearby Crest Fishery employed many local workers, and the Hotel Crest filled the need for necessary lodging. Many island towns borrowed the well-known name "Beach Haven" in naming their communities, as evidenced in the names of Beach Haven Crest, Beach Haven Terrace, Beach Haven Gardens, and Haven Beach.

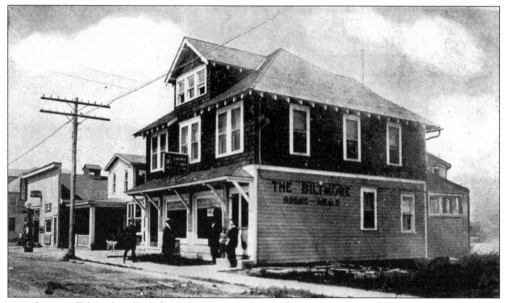

Another small hotel, called the Biltmore, was located on Bay Avenue in Beach Haven. Clean rooms and good meals were a specialty. Next door to the hotel was an old gas station and automotive repair garage.

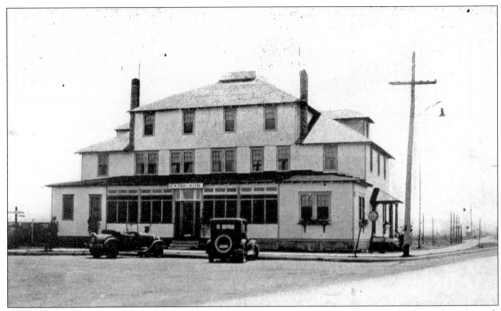

One of the oldest and most continually operated hotels in the area was the Ockanickon Hotel, which, after 1931, was renamed Wida's. Built in 1926 on the Boulevard in Brant Beach, it quickly became a local landmark.

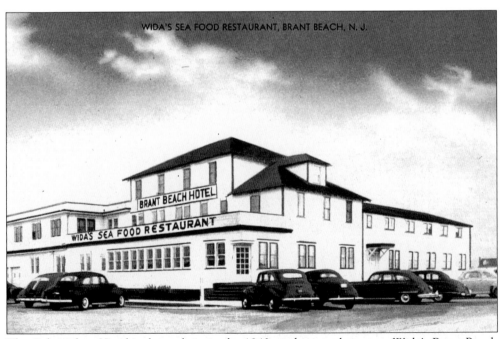

The Ockanickon Hotel is shown here in the 1940s and is now known as Wida's Brant Beach Hotel and Sea Food Restaurant. With its familiar green exterior, the family-run operation remains today in the very same location.

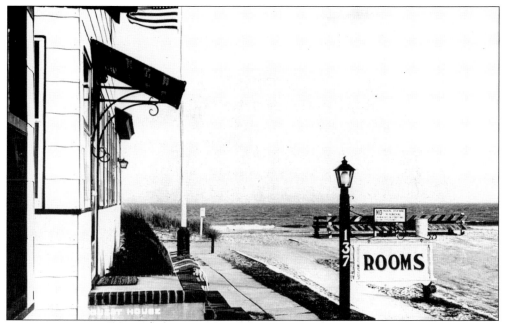

Many small guesthouses dotted the island. Most were simply furnished rooms as part of a larger private residence. Shown here is a simple oceanside lodging on 18th Street in Ship Bottom.

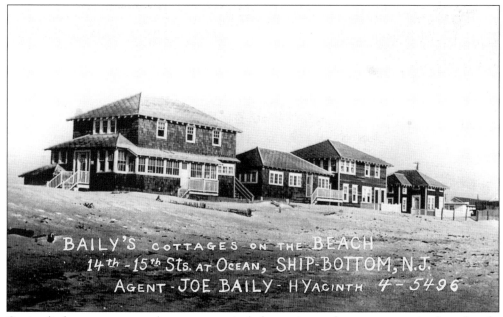

BAILY'S COTTAGES ON THE BEACH
14th - 15th Sts. AT Ocean, SHIP-BOTTOM, N.J.
AGENT - JOE BAILY - HYACINTH 4 - 5496

Quaint little cottages were also an economical alternative to the more expensive large hotels. Bailey's Cottages on the Beach was a great place to enjoy the summer on the oceanfront.

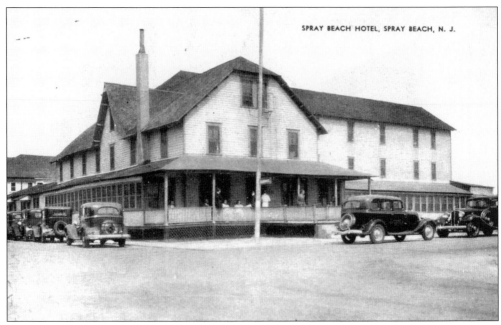

SPRAY BEACH HOTEL, SPRAY BEACH, N. J.

Philadelphia mortgage banker William Ringgold built a large house on a plot of land called Cranberry Hill in 1889. Around his home, tiny cottages sprung up and the area was named Spray Beach. He later enlarged his home into the Spray Beach Hotel shown here. The hotel was torn down c. 1969 to make way for a new motel.

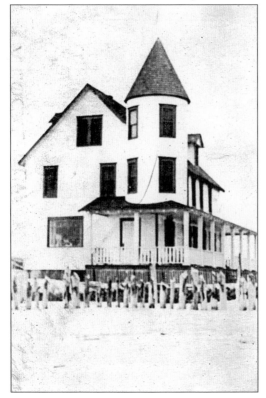

A stay on LBI could also have been spent in a guesthouse. This particular one was located on the ocean at 12th Street in Surf City. It was originally called Great Swamp, but the town later changed its name to the more attractive Surf City.

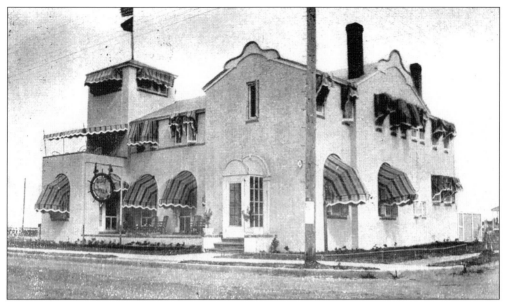

Hotels each had their own individual style or character. The Surfvilla, a 1920s-era hotel located on 16th Street in Surf City, took on a Spanish flair.

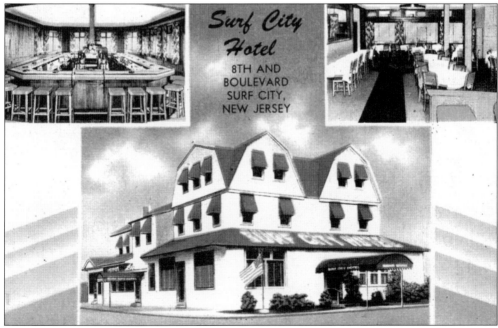

Built in 1884 and originally called the Mansion House, this building was moved to the ocean side of Eighth Street and the Boulevard in Surf City. It was renamed the Long Beach Inn and was later renamed the Marquette Hotel. The hotel was sold again c. 1920 and became the Surf City Hotel.

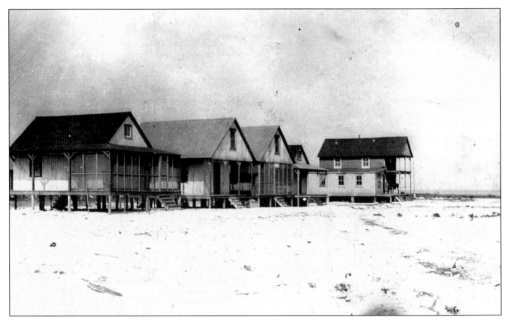

The small town of High Point is located near Harvey Cedars. This area, used for camping and fishing, attracted visitors who built small bungalows along the beach. Pictured here are such structures.

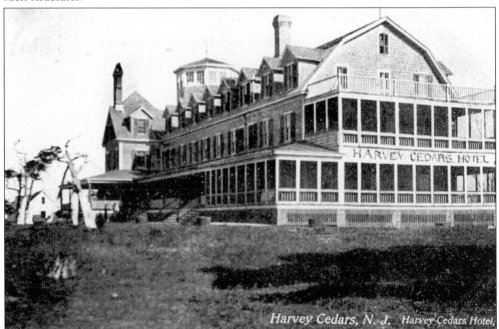

Built originally as a home in 1812, the building was bought by Samuel Perrine of Barnegat in 1841 with plans to open a hotel. Perrine enlarged the old wooden building and renamed it the Connahassett House at Harvey Cedars. The hotel was later known as the Harvey Cedars Hotel. The hotel was sold in 1881, sold in 1920, and sold again in 1921, becoming the YMCA's Camp Whelen. In 1941, it would change hands one final time and become the Harvey Cedar Bible Conference complex.

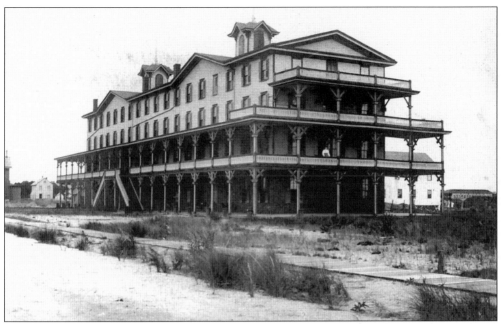

Located in popular Barnegat City was the large Oceanic Hotel. Built by Benjamin Franklin Archer of Camden in 1881, it possessed many unique characteristics, such as rooftop cupolas, wide porches, and airy rooms. Located at East Fourth Street and the ocean in Barnegat City, the hotel was moved back away from the water's edge several times, an amazing feat for such a large structure.

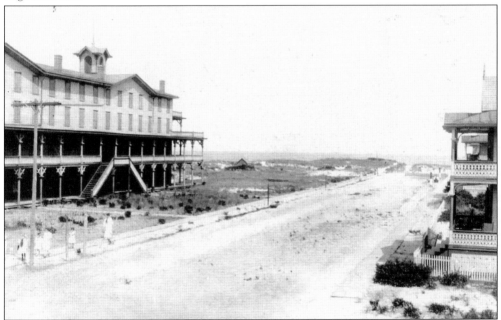

An outbreak of typhoid fever hit the hotel hard in 1910, with one young woman dying of the disease. It was later rumored that dead rats had been found in the hotel drinking water tanks housed in the cupolas on top of the building. The hotel closed in 1914 and was destroyed in the storm of 1920.

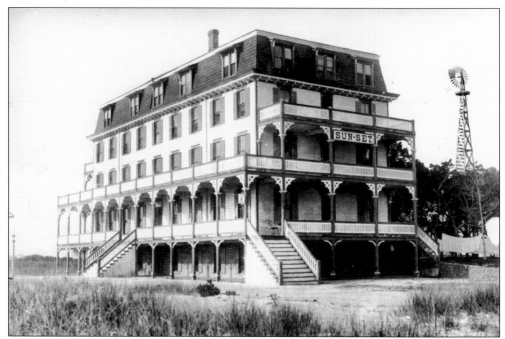

Another hotel built in Barnegat City was called the Sans Souci. Constructed *c*. 1882, the hotel was later renamed the Sunset. Located on the bay front, it contained over 150 rooms. The Sunset was one of a few year-round resorts, catering primarily to hunters during the winter season. The hotel remained prosperous through the 1930s until it burned to the ground on the night of June 26, 1932.

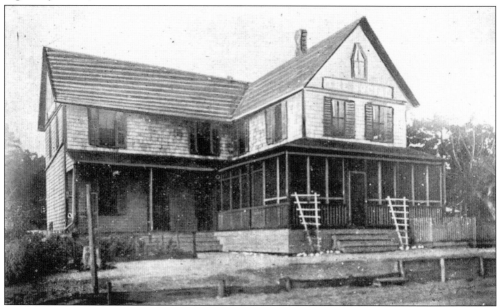

Shown here is the hotel known as the Social. It was built in Barnegat City in 1885 by William C. Kroeger and his wife. After Kroeger died in 1891, his wife continued to run the old hotel for many more years. In 1915, she sold the hotel, and later, the building was operated as a restaurant and rooming house until *c*. 1953.

Six
TRANSPORTATION

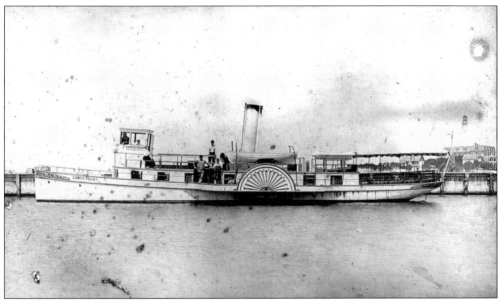

This rare photograph of the paddle-wheel steamer *Connetquoit* was probably taken at the Barnegat City steamer dock in 1885. The dock was located on the upper end of Broadway, just north of the Sunset. The boat ran during the summer months and shuttled passengers from the Pennsylvania Railroad station at the Barnegat Pier (located on the south shore of Toms River) to Seaside and then on to Barnegat City. Departing guests would then board a horsecar for a short trip to the various local hotels. Steamboat service to the island began *c.* 1872 and continued for just a few short years. In the distance on the right is the familiar Barnegat Lighthouse.

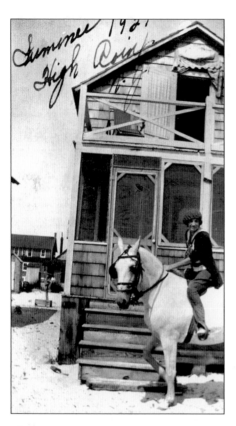

Getting around the island in the early days of its development meant either walking or riding a horse. Much later, the railroads and the automobiles would come, making travel much easier. Here, Florence Hartnett (the grandmother of the author) saddles up at High Point for a trip into town. Florence Hartnett delivered mail on Mayor J. B. Kinsey's horse c. 1921.

The Wharf.   Beach Haven, N. J.

Before the trains and automobiles came to the island, many visitors also took boats to and from the island. Travel could be unpredictable in the winter months, and regular schedules were hard to keep.

It was not until June 1886 that the railroad built a line across the Barnegat Bay to Long Beach Island. Passengers could now board a train in Philadelphia or New York and, after a lengthy trip, cross over onto LBI via the Pennsylvania Railroad line. Shown here are early ticket stubs for a trip to Beach Haven.

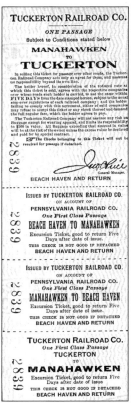

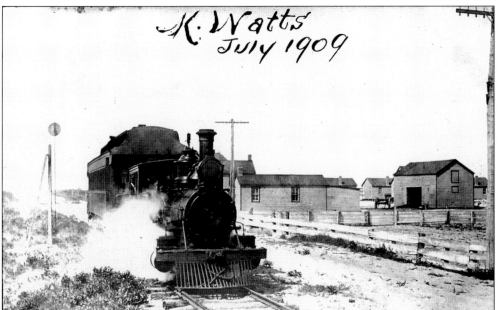

Once onto the island, passengers could board the Manahawkin and Long Beach Railroad and travel from Barnegat City south to Beach Haven. Owned by the Pennsylvania Railroad, the operation of the rails was contracted out to the Tuckerton Railroad. An early steam locomotive is seen here *c.* 1909, chugging along the sandy trails near Harvey Cedars.

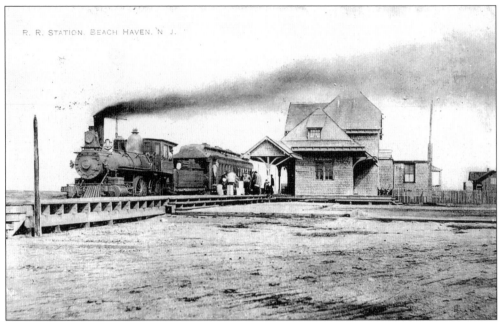

The station at Beach Haven was completed in 1886, and the first engine and passenger cars rolled into town on July 24 of that same year. Hotel guests could arrive in style aboard the train and be greeted at the station by hotel representatives.

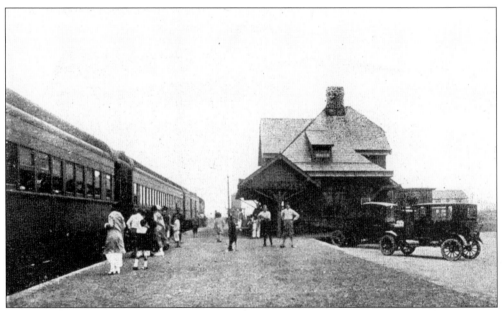

Early automobiles await passengers at the Pennsylvania Railroad station at Beach Haven. Once the trains reached the end of the line at either Beach Haven or Barnegat City, they were backed up and turned around on a spur in the meadows.

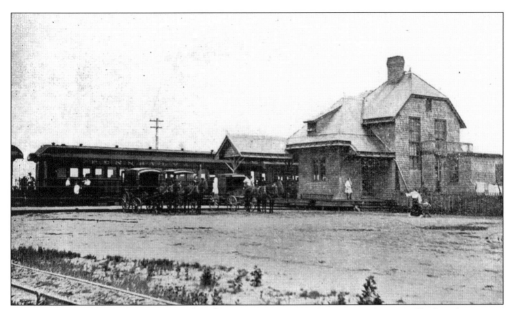

Horse-drawn jitneys pick up and drop off guests at the Beach Haven station. This lovely station was located at Third Street and Delaware Avenue in Beach Haven.

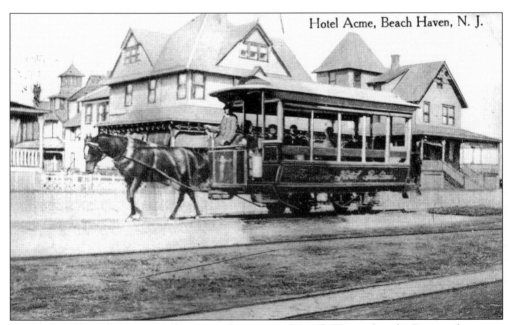

A Hotel Baldwin horsecar trolley passes by a row of Beach Haven hotels. During this time, there was no real direct road running the length of the island, and most streets were dirt-covered roadways.

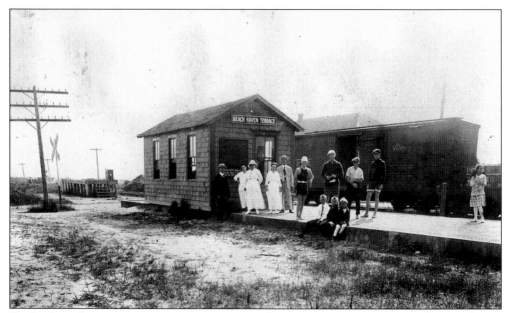

Finely dressed passengers await a train at Beach Haven Terrace *c.* 1923. The people are identified on the back of the image as Mr. and Mrs. Vogt, Mrs. Seitter, Mr. and Mrs. Pierce, James, the three Osbourne boys, the three Shaeffer children, and Eleanor Haines. Old wooden freight cars can be seen in the background.

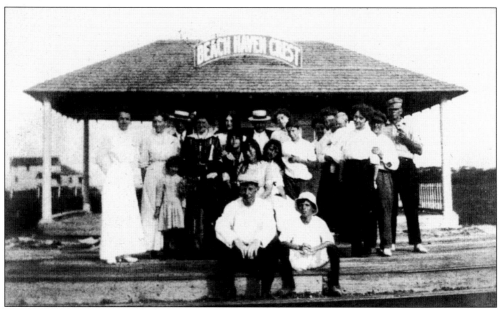

Another group of passengers poses for a photograph at Beach Haven Crest. This small open-air station was one of many along the length of the Manahawkin and Long Beach line.

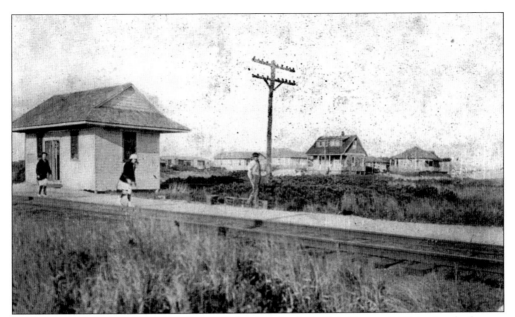

A small wooden station stands at Beach Arlington (today's Ship Bottom). This view looks east toward the ocean *c.* 1922.

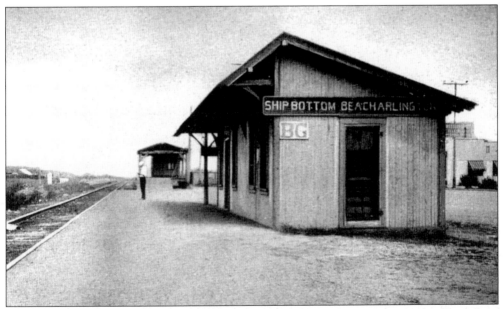

This train station once stood at 23rd Street in Beach Arlington, opposite the lumberyards of the Conrad Brothers Lumber Company. The older name of the town, Beach Arlington, is used here in conjunction with its new name, Ship Bottom.

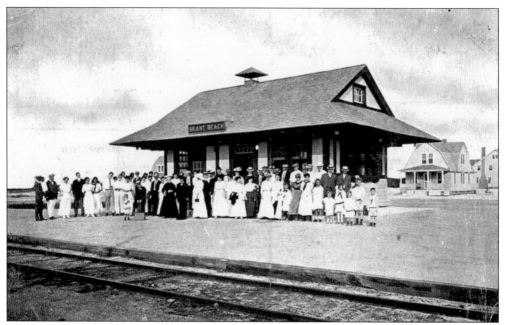

This attractive station, shown here while new in 1913, was built at Stanton Avenue in Brant Beach. It was used until *c.* 1935 and was later moved and converted to a residential home located around 60th Street.

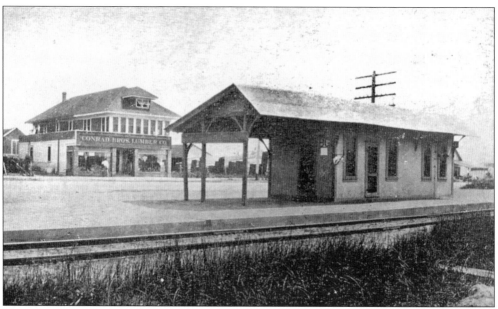

The Conrad Brothers Lumber Company provided much of the materials for the building boom on LBI. Its location is shown here, across the street from the train station at Ship Bottom.

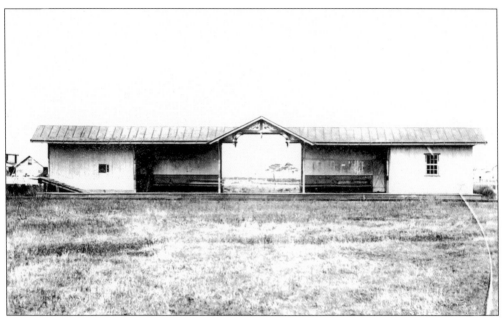

A fairly large wooden station was built for passengers at Harvey Cedars on the northern end of the island. Railroad freight service also existed on the island but was not as profitable as the passenger service. This view was taken *c.* 1909.

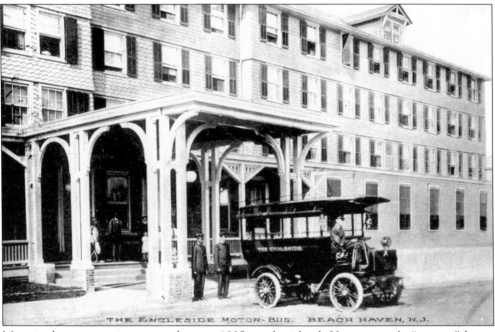

Motorized transportation came about *c.* 1905 on the island. Here, an early "autocar" bus is attended to by Hotel Engleside porters. It replaced the earlier horsecars as the preferred means of transportation to and from the hotels.

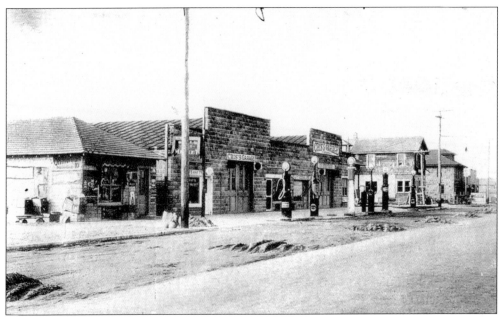

Automobiles would not be commonplace on the island until the opening of the causeway bridge in 1914. But some early automobiles were transported via train to the island prior to its opening. These marvels of technology required both maintenance and of course fuel to run on. Small service stations such as this one at Ship Bottom served their needs.

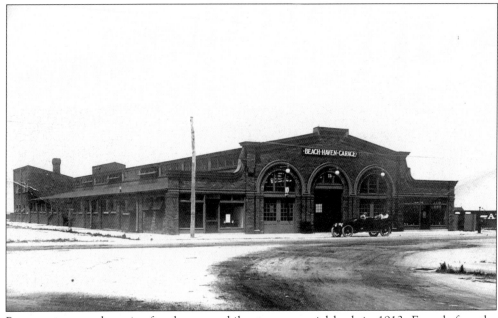

Proper storage and repair of early automobiles were essential back in 1913. Even before the bridge to the mainland was built, Frederick Ostendorff had foresight and built a garage at Beach Haven. Able to hold over 200 automobiles, it protected them from both the rain and the damaging salt air.

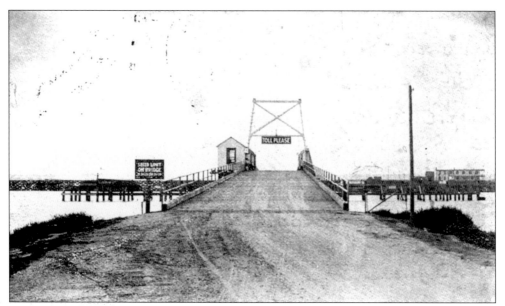

Many automobiles crossed the new causeway bridge after its opening in 1914. A toll booth was added, as shown here, to collect revenue. Years later, the tolls were eliminated.

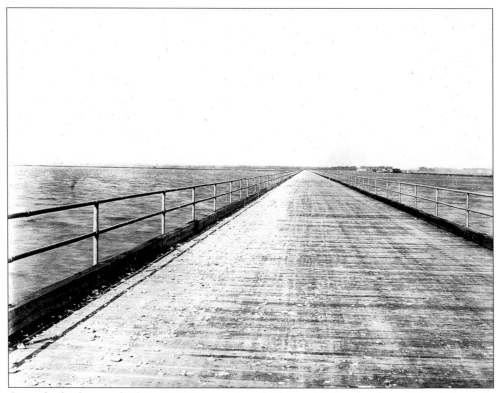

Once the bridge was built in 1914, its wooden planks rumbled under the weight of the early automobiles. Sea shells, dropped by seagulls overhead, were a common enemy of the balloon tire, and the bridge was swept often to avoid costly tire blowouts.

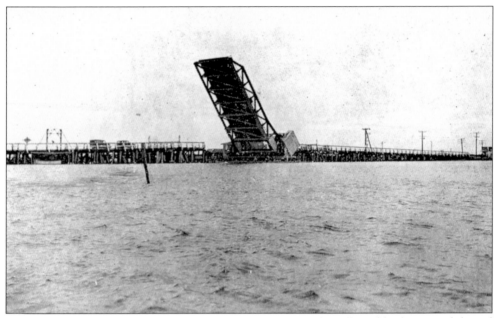

The drawbridge shown here replaced an earlier swing span that allowed both automobile and boat traffic to alternately pass.

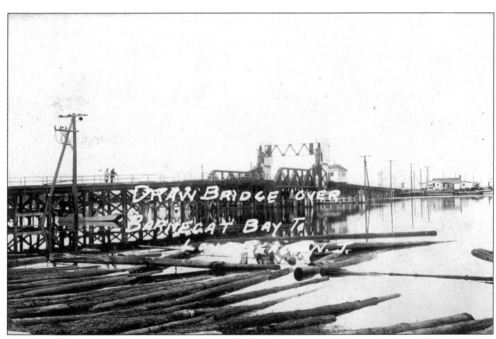

Another sharp image shows the newer bascule drawbridge over the bay. Many people remember the wooden causeway bridge, remaining in place from 1914 until 1959, when it was replaced with a new concrete span.

Seven
SPECIAL EVENTS

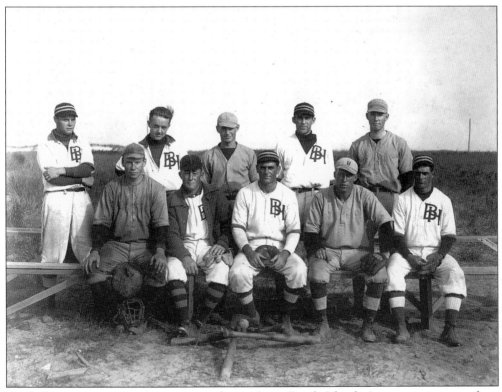

Baseball as a summer pastime was popular on Long Beach Island. A community team from Beach Haven was formed early on and played other local teams in organized games. Even the hotels sponsored friendly games in the streets, often including both men and women.

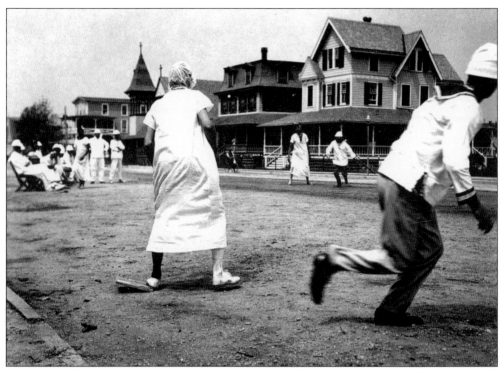

Here, men in dresses compete in a friendly game of baseball in the streets of Beach Haven. The men were required to wear the dresses in order to even the odds when playing with and sometimes against the women.

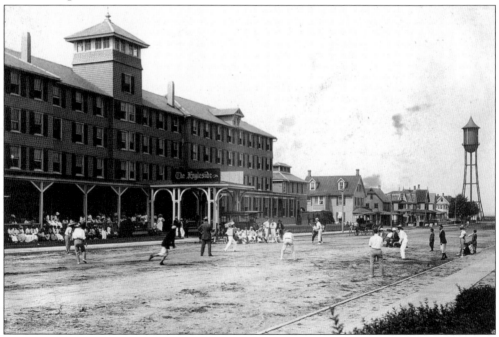

A game of ball is played outside the Engleside Hotel c. 1914. Play would have to stop for the occasional horse and wagon to pass by. Note the old water tower at the end of the street.

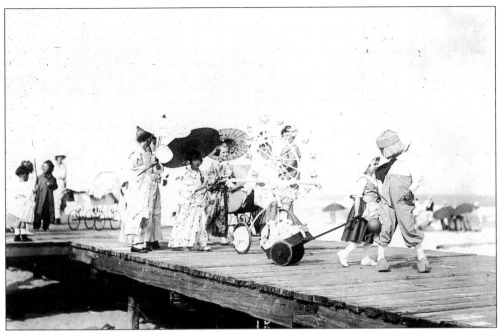

Baby parades were a popular event in most seaside resorts such as Atlantic City and Asbury Park. Not to be outdone, Beach Haven also held its own event. Here, a group of young children dresses in costumes and parades along the Beach Haven boardwalk.

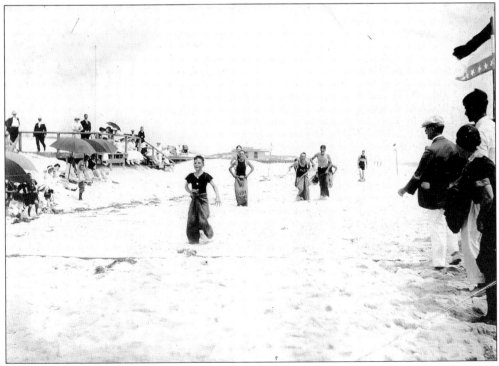

The beach was home to many holiday celebrations and other events. Competitions such as sack races, tug of war, and others provided fun for all.

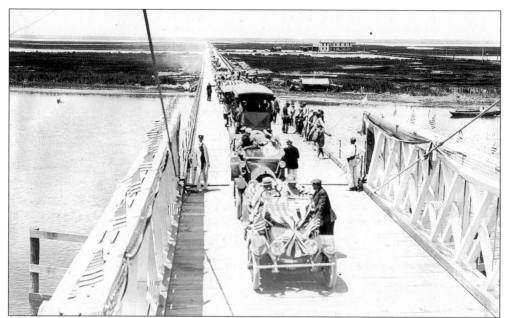

On June 20, 1914, the newly built causeway bridge over the Barnegat Bay was opened to traffic. A simple ribbon cutting was not enough. A huge island-wide celebration was planned, and a grand automobile procession was held. Early cars came from near and far, decorated with flags, banners, and streamers. Here, Governor Fielder leads the way in a flag-draped vehicle.

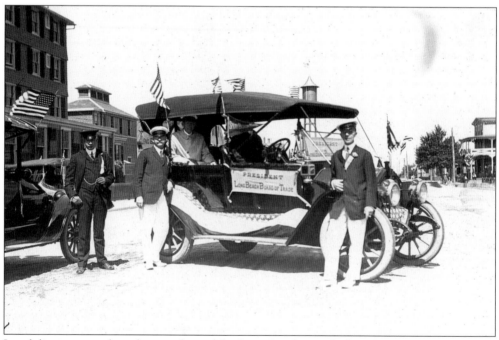

Local dignitaries such as the president of the Long Beach Board of Trade were on hand for the bridge dedication. The day was filled with speeches, music, and celebration, topped off by a game of baseball between the Beach Haven team and another team from nearby Tuckerton on the mainland.

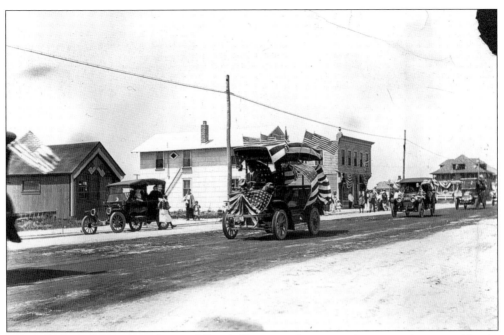

Cars roll along the Boulevard toward Beach Haven in this image. Souvenir plaques and books were given to automobile entries, which competed for the best decoration. Local residents decorated their homes along the route and also competed for awards as well.

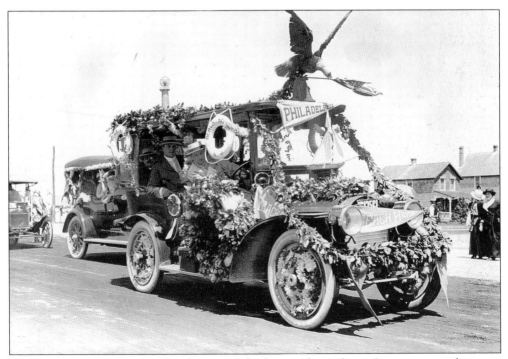

Some vehicles were decorated with unusual displays, as shown here. Ornaments on this entry included a large eagle atop the roof, flowers, various pennants, life preservers, and even a model of the Barnegat Light at the rear.

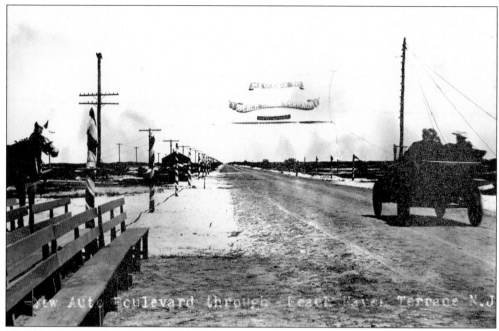

The bleachers and viewing stands still remain at Beach Haven Terrace even after the celebration has ended. A banner overhead reads, "Welcome to Beach Haven Terrace."

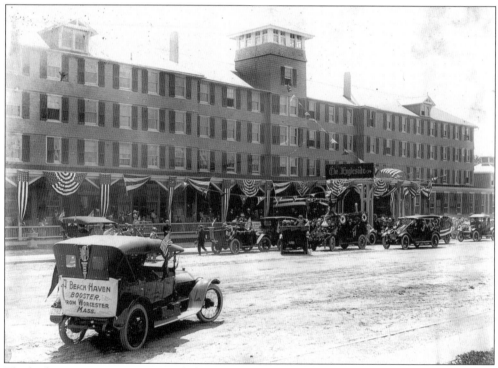

The bridge-opening procession ended at the Engleside Hotel in Beach Haven, where a full day of festivities began. The hotel itself was decorated in colorful bunting to celebrate the occasion.

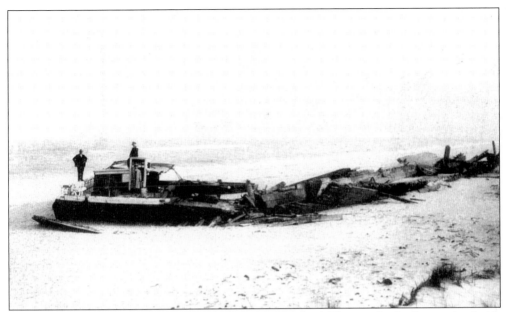

Shipwrecks were an unfortunate event on Long Beach Island. The wreck of a ship on the shoals brought crowds of curious onlookers. After the crew was rescued, all efforts were made to salvage any cargo aboard the ship. Often the lumber from what remained of the vessel was taken by the locals and used in the construction of homes and buildings. This image shows the wreck of the *Cecil P. Stewart* at Surf City.

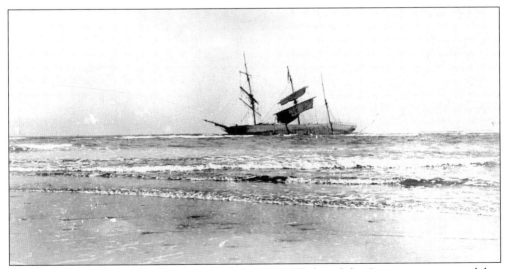

Here, a bark founders at the Barnegat shoals in 1912. All aboard the *Caterina* were rescued, but both the cargo and the ship were lost.

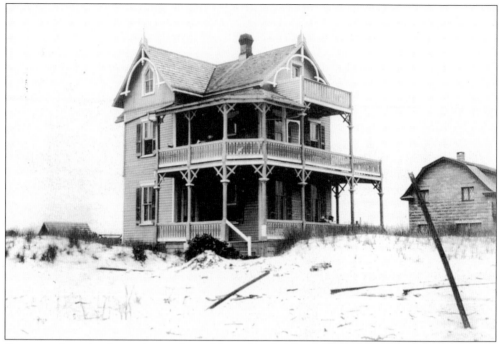

Storms and erosion have always plagued Long Beach Island. Things were no different back in 1920. Here, a beautiful Victorian home at Barnegat City is shown just before the looming storm.

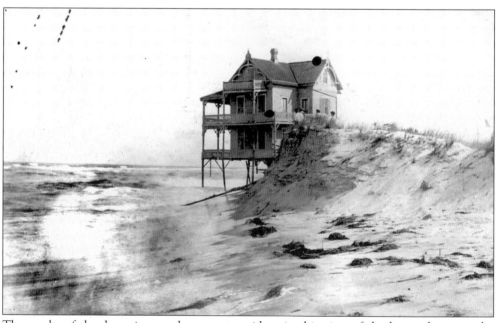

The results of the damaging northeaster are evident in this view of the home shown in the previous photograph. The sand has been eroded away from the foundation, and the house now sits precariously at the ocean's edge.

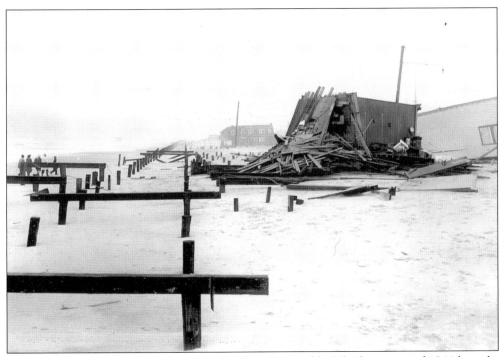

Events such as storms and hurricanes are truly unforgettable. The hurricane of 1944 brought great destruction to the island. High winds, damaging rain, and high tides ravaged the island. The once beautiful boardwalk at Beach Haven is shown here after the storm.

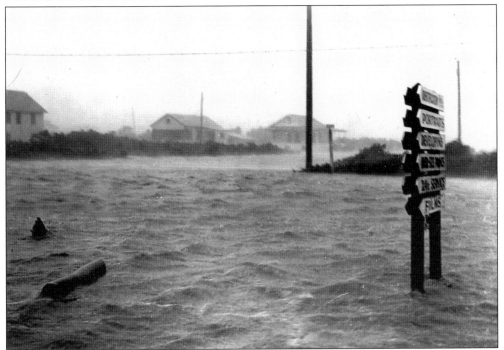

Many local landmarks such as the fishing piers, several beach pavilions, the pound fisheries, the boardwalk, and many homes were completely destroyed in the wake of the storm.

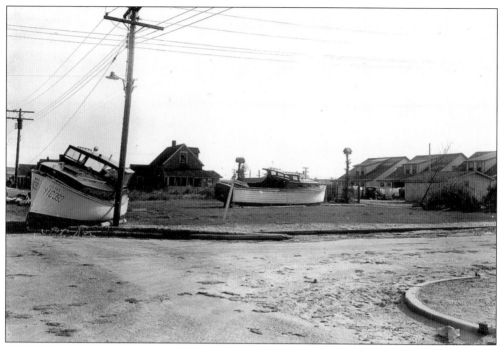

Boats were washed ashore by the hurricane winds and high tides. Here, they sit in yards and on street corners. Cleanup lasted several weeks, with much sand having to be removed from streets to make them passable again. Five people drowned during the 1944 hurricane.

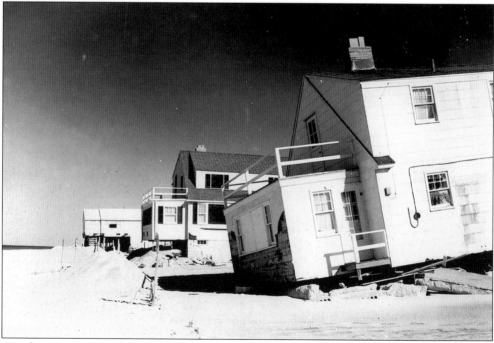

Another great storm struck LBI back in March 1962, leaving destruction throughout the island. Hardest hit was Harvey Cedars, the narrowest part of the island, where the waters of the ocean came together to meet the Barnegat Bay.

Eight
CHURCH AND
COMMUNITY

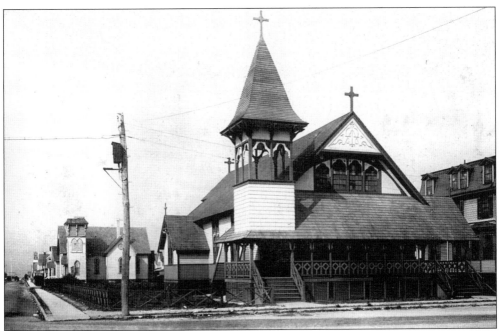

Long Beach Island was home to many religious faiths. Beautiful houses of worship were built throughout the island. This building, built in 1881 and located at Engleside and Beach Avenues in Beach Haven, housed the Holy Innocents Church. In the distance is the Methodist church.

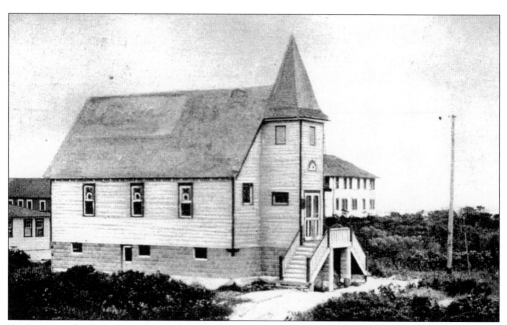

Every town had its own local church. This community church was located in tiny Beach Haven Crest.

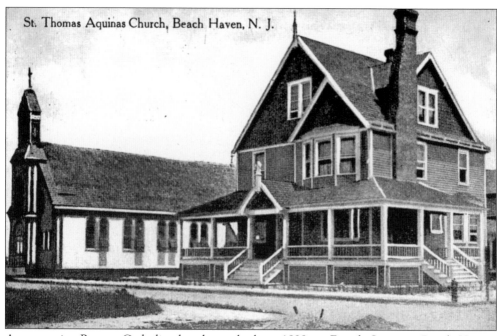

St. Thomas Aquinas Church, Beach Haven, N. J.

An attractive Roman Catholic church was built in 1899 on Fourth Street in Beach Haven. Called the Church of St. Thomas Aquinas, it was a mission as well.

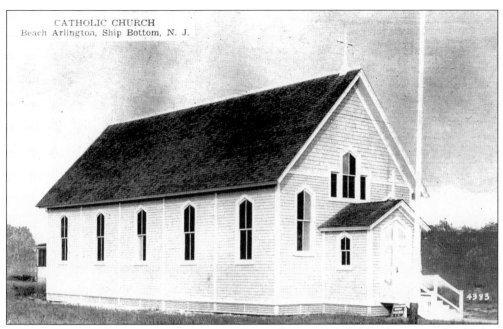

A typical shore-style church is shown at Surf City (here mislabeled by the postcard publisher as Beach Arlington, Ship Bottom).

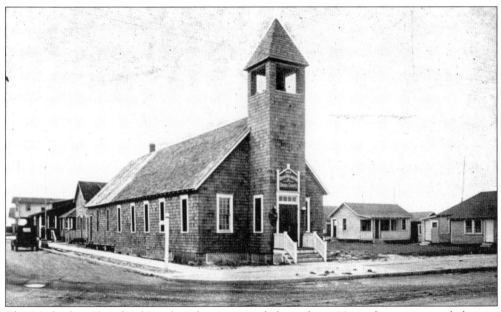

The Methodist Church of Beach Arlington was dedicated in 1924 and was commonly known as the Union church. Before it was built, residents met for services at the old Beach Arlington train station on 19th Street.

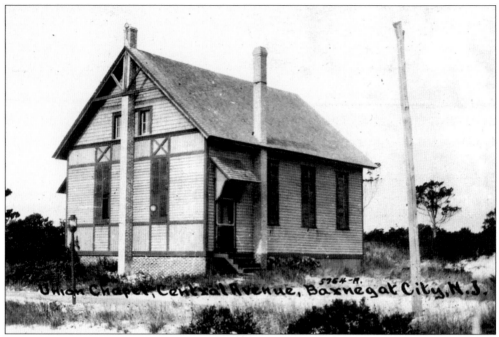

The old Union Chapel stood on Central Avenue in Barnegat City since 1890. Throughout its history, it was a Methodist, Presbyterian, and Episcopalian church. The back of this image reads, "This is the little chapel of Barnegat City, where all the good people of the town worship."

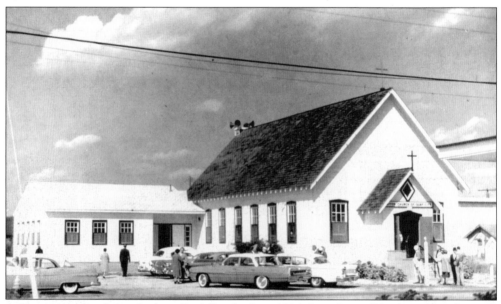

A Protestant church was built in Surf City back in 1934. It is shown here located at Seventh Street and Central Avenue in Surf City. As with many other congregations, members met in fire halls and town centers until funds could be raised to build a church.

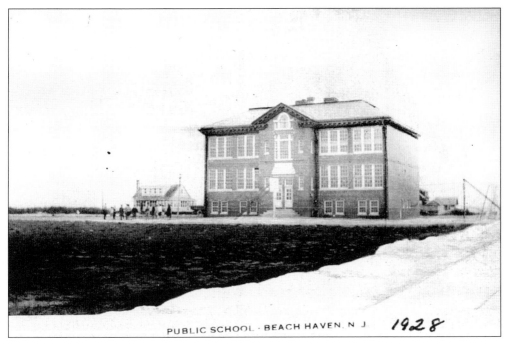

PUBLIC SCHOOL · BEACH HAVEN. N J   *1928*

Early on, many grade-school children from LBI were educated in small one-room schoolhouses. One such schoolhouse was begun in 1904 in Harvey Cedars. Most high school students traveled to the mainland in Barnegat to attend classes there. This particular school was built in 1912 on Eighth Street in Beach Haven and is shown here *c.* 1928. Other schools were located in Barnegat City and later in Ship Bottom.

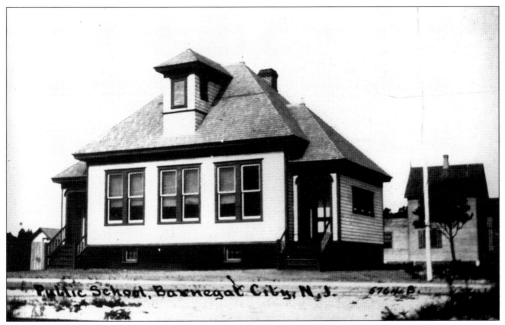

The schoolhouse at Barnegat City, built in 1904, remained in use until 1951. It was later restored and used as the present-day home of the Barnegat Light Historical Museum.

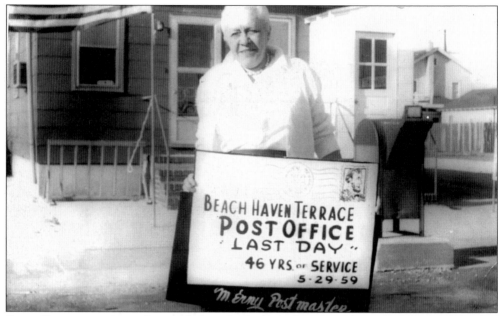

Post offices were scattered around the island, often found inside general stores and other businesses. Here, the Beach Haven Terrace office celebrates its final day of service after 46 years of duty.

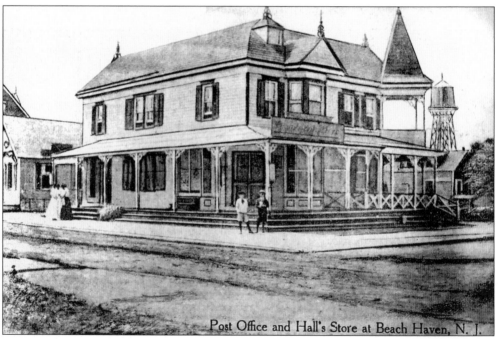

A trip to the store meant buying needed goods, swapping gossip, and picking up the day's mail. The post office was located inside Hall's Store in Beach Haven.

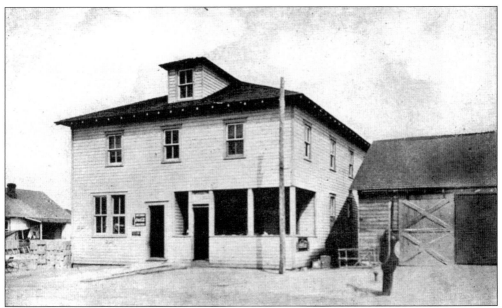

Pictured here is the old post office at Beach Arlington. Most people picked up their mail, as delivery was not yet widely implemented on the island.

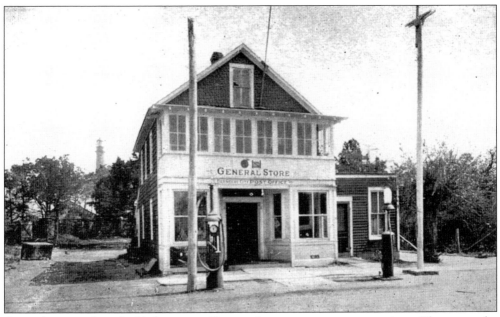

General stores often doubled as post offices and sometimes even gas stations. They were the forerunners of today's convenience stores. Note the old glass-top gas pumps out front.

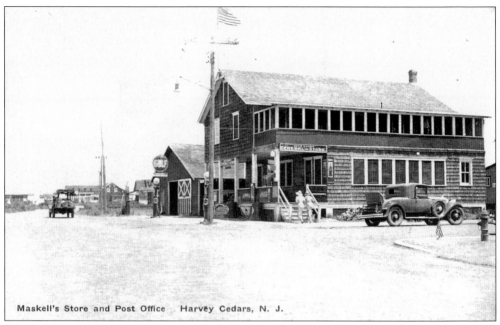

Maskell's Store and Post Office   Harvey Cedars, N. J.

A popular spot in Harvey Cedars was Maskell's Store. Inside could be found the local post office as well as goods of all kinds. The building was built *c.* 1910 at 79th Street and the Boulevard by J. B. Kinsey.

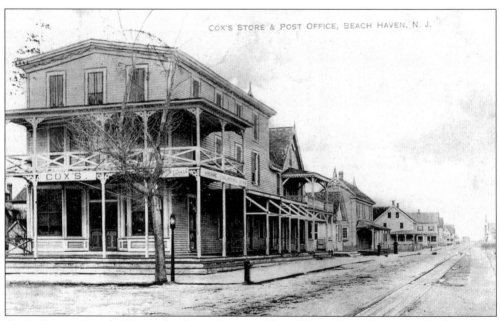

COX'S STORE & POST OFFICE, BEACH HAVEN, N. J.

Cox's Store at Beach Haven also housed a post office. This early view shows the three-story wooden structure on Beach Avenue. The trolley ran along Beach Avenue to the old Beach Haven railroad station.

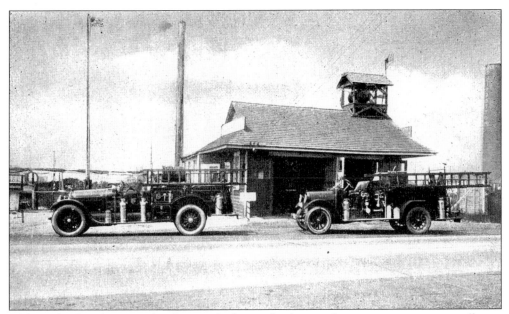

Old wooden hotels meant the chance of a fire, and volunteer fire companies sprung up all over the island to battle such blazes. The Ship Bottom Beach Arlington Fire Company No. 1 is shown at its station *c.* 1932.

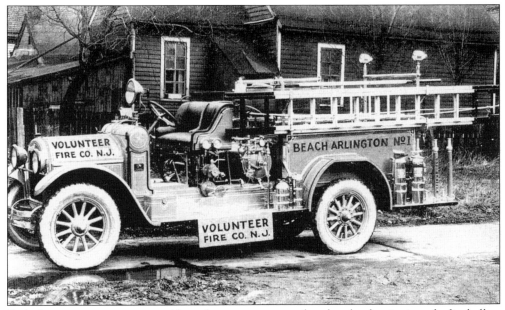

Early fire apparatus was manned by volunteers summoned to duty by the ringing of a fire bell or siren. Pictured is an early vehicle from the Beach Arlington fire station.

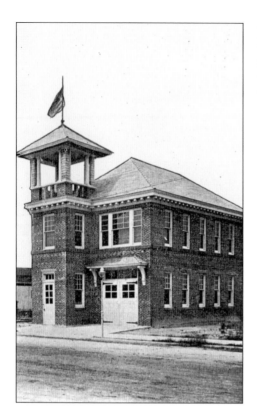

Due to the greater population of Beach Haven, the town had a large company of volunteers always ready to assist in putting out fires. This view, taken around the mid-1920s, shows its two-story brick building with tall fire tower.

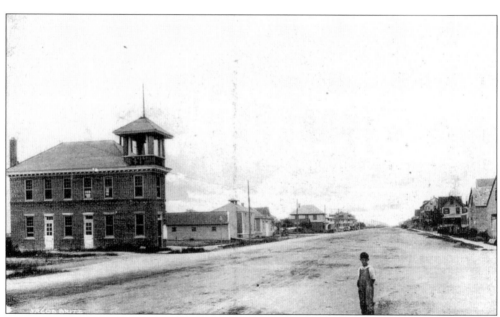

Here is another view of the same fire station at Beach Haven. Years later, the building was enlarged and the tower was removed.

Nine

BUSINESS AND ENTERTAINMENT

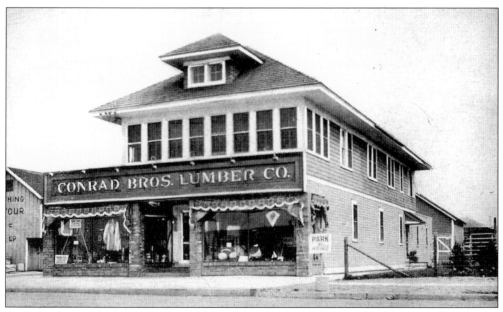

Businesses were the heart of many LBI towns. They provided goods, services, and often the news of the day. Other businesses provided food, drink, or entertainment. The Conrad Brothers Lumber Company is shown here at 23rd Street in Ship Bottom.

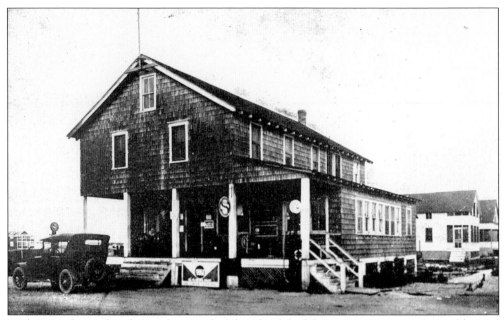

High Point, located at the northern end of the island, had few stores. Most people would travel to busy Beach Haven for shopping. Shown here is the general store at High Point.

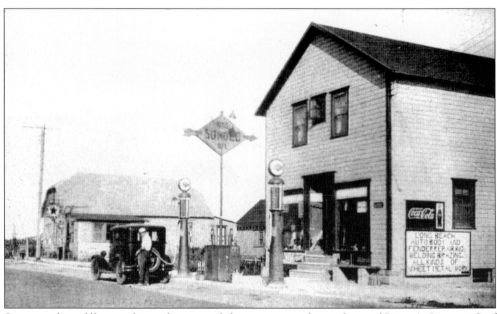

Stopping for a fill-up in his early automobile, a man stands out front of Reiser's Store at Surf City. The store also provided auto body repairs and welding, as shown on the billboard.

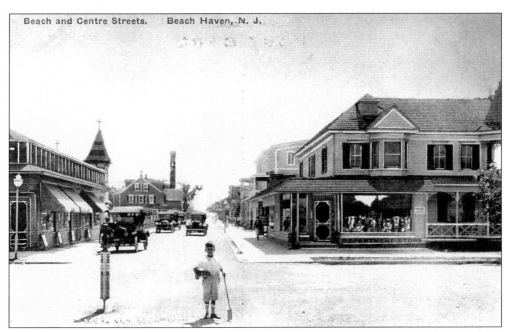

A more modern shopping district is shown here in Beach Haven. Rows of stores sold everything from dresses to prescription drugs. A small boy stands in the middle of the street with his new sand pail and shovel.

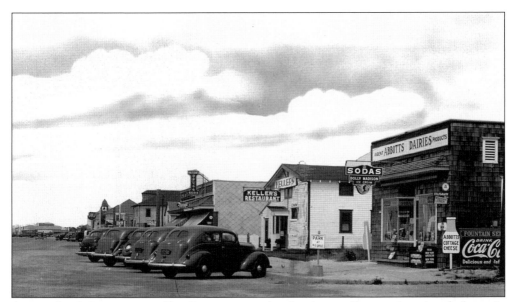

A row of early businesses in Ship Bottom catered to locals as well as tourists. A soda fountain in the store on the right was a popular hangout in the 1940s. Next door was Keller's Restaurant and farther down the street the drugstore.

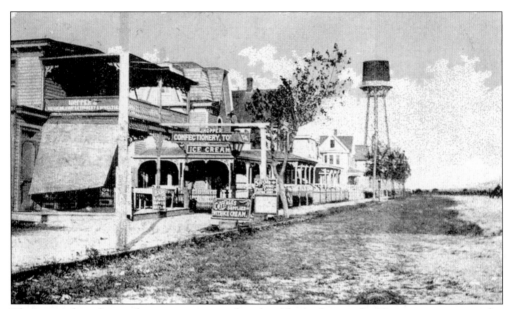

There is nothing better than ice cream on a hot day. Shown here is the Hopper ice-cream parlor on Old South Avenue in Beach Haven. They sold all types of ice cream, confectioneries, novelties, and even baseballs and bats, according to the sign posted out front.

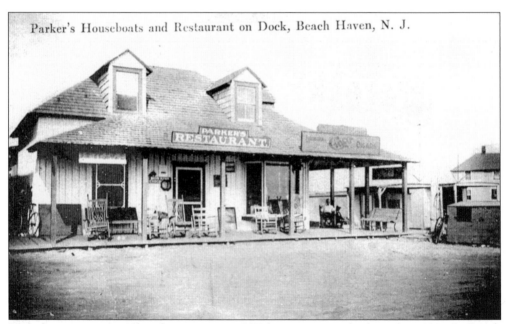

Houseboats were a popular place to stay on LBI beginning way back in the 1880s. In Beach Haven, these small boats provided the comforts of home while travelers enjoyed the sights and sounds of the bay and meadows. They were both sold and rented from Parker's Houseboats and Restaurant, shown here. The houseboat colonies were later banned by a town ordinance in 1926 due to health concerns.

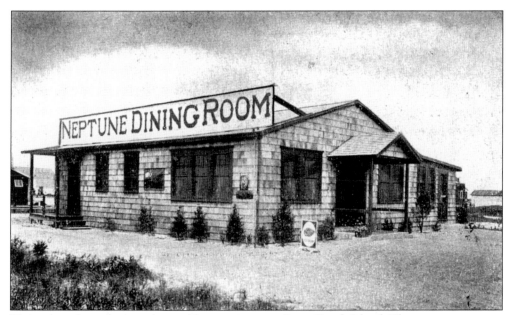

Dining has always been a pleasurable experience on Long Beach Island. The many restaurants throughout the island specialized in the freshest of seafood. This was the case at the Neptune Dining Room at High Point, shown c. 1931.

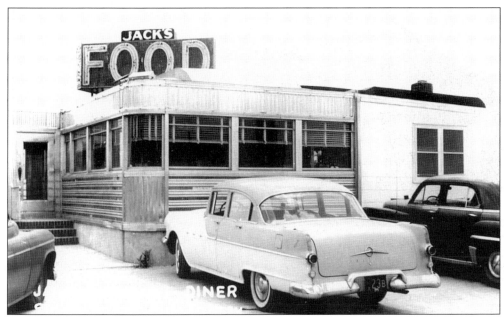

A meal at Jack's Deluxe Diner was always a treat. Located in Ship Bottom, it quickly became a favorite of locals and tourists looking for a quick bite to eat. Pictured here in the 1950s, it was one of a few chrome diners on the island.

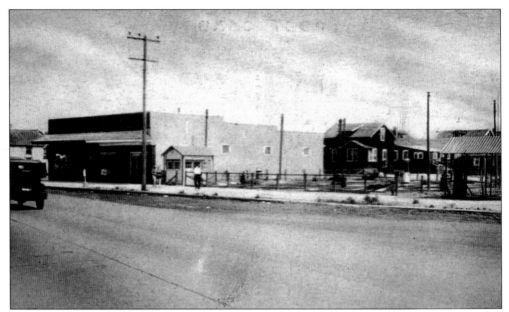

Long Beach Island never had an amusement pier like Atlantic City, Point Pleasant, or Seaside. But after a fun day at the beach, one could spend the evening playing a round of miniature golf at one of the island's several miniature courses like this one at Beach Arlington.

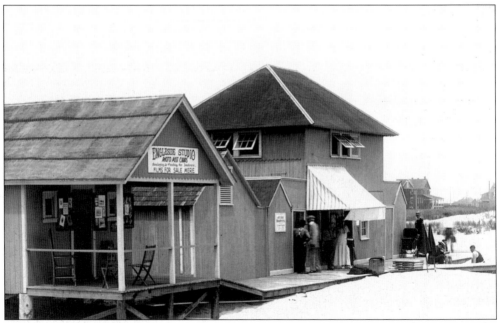

A trip to LBI would not be complete without a souvenir. Studio photographs were popular keepsakes, and studios such as this one allowed customers to pose for the camera. They also catered to amateurs who took their own photographs by developing them and sometimes printing them into real-photo postcards. This is a rare image of the Engleside Studio in Beach Haven *c.* 1910.

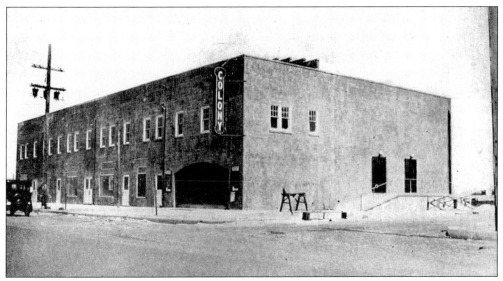

Movies were a great escape from the summer heat. Two theaters were built on the island by a developer named Harry Colmer. This theater, built in the late 1920s, was located in Brant Beach on 35th Street. In the 1930s, the innovative Colmer used large cakes of ice and powerful fans to cool down the theater for performances.

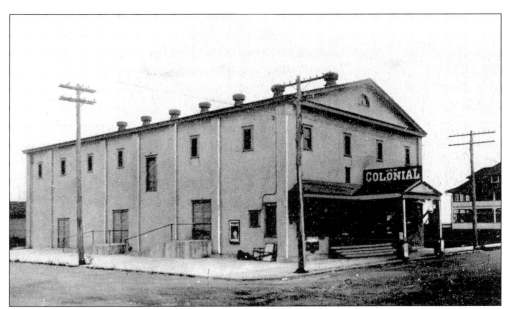

Colmer's other theater, built in 1922, was located in Beach Haven on Bay Avenue and Centre Street. There one could experience the latest silent movie to the music of a piano player.

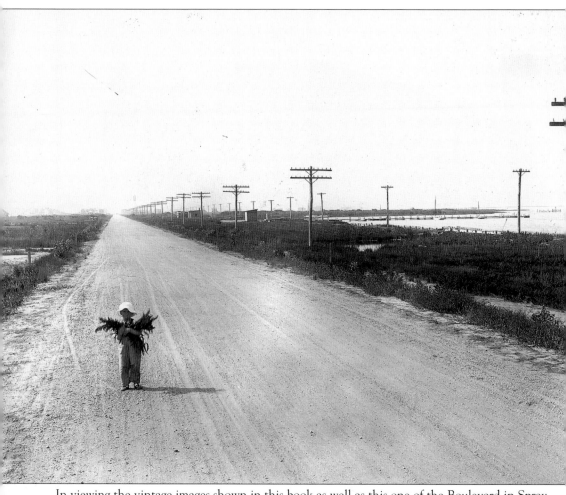

In viewing the vintage images shown in this book as well as this one of the Boulevard in Spray Beach *c.* 1914, we remember the simpler times, days gone by, and the incredible beauty of Long Beach Island, a treasure of the Jersey Shore.